Use LibreOffice Base

THOMAS ECCLESTONE

ISBN: **1502941708**
ISBN-13: **978-1502941701**

NONFICTION BOOKS BY AUTHOR

Celestia 1.6 Beginners Guide
Use LibreOffice Writer: A Beginners Guide
Use LibreOffice Impress: A Beginners Guide
Use LibreOffice Base: A Beginners Guide
Use Podio: To Manage A Small Company

CONTENTS

DEDICATION

This book is dedicated to Dean Wesley Smith for all his help.

1 GETTING STARTED – CREATING A TABLE

What is LibreOffice Base?

LibreOffice Base is a program supplied with the LibreOffice Productivity Suite that allows you to create, manage and run databases. In many ways it's similar to Access although it is free and provides you with the ability to record information such as:

- Company address books
- Inventory
- Time sheet information
- Employee records

Or almost anything else that you can think of.

LibreOffice Base also interfaces with larger databases systems such as Oracle, Microsoft SQL Server, or MySQL. Because of this ability as your company grows the systems that you create in LibreOffice Base can grow without change being obvious to the end user.

Best of all, when you're a small company you don't really want to spend a lot of money on database systems. LibreOffice Base is a free solution that had most of the functionality of programs that are much more expensive to use.

What is a Database?

Throughout this book we're going to use some difficult terminology, so I'll try to explain it while I'm going along. One of the first things you need to understand is the idea of a database. In simple terms a database is like a set of file draws. You can store all the information you need on a subject in the database and then retrieve it.

The analogy doesn't go quite as far as the reality, though, because you can also run automatic queries – or, in other words, questions- on the information you store in a database that can provide more information for your company.

For example, if you were running a small café shop you might record not only the staff wages and hours, but also the staff lunches and training you do for staff. By running a query you can find out not only the salary cost of a particular employee but also the actual cost of employing them. This is new information derived from other information that your company already stores.

Database: An organised collection of information that your company holds about a subject

Query: A question that your company wants to answer by accessing the information in a database.

Obviously as you use LibreOffice you'll learn more about these concepts but for now that's a good enough start!

Tutorial: Your First Database.

In this tutorial we're going to create a simple staff database. It's not going to be particularly useful, but we're going to record:

- **Employee Number**
- **Staff name**
- **Telephone Number**
- **Address**

The Database Wizard

When you open up LibreOffice Base by clicking on the

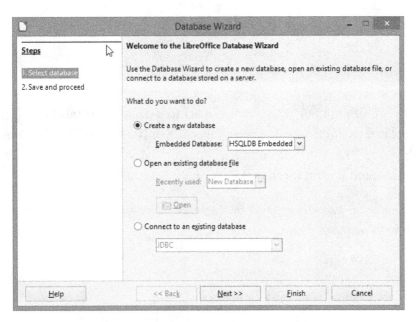

tile in the windows start page it will take you immediately to the Database Wizard:

Note that there are three options on this screen:

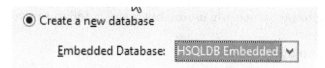

We're going to use this option first. When you're using LibreOffice Base as a standalone desktop app you only need to create an embedded database. If you want to use a database like MySQL you'd connected to an existing database.

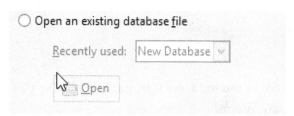

This option allows you to open a database that you've already created.

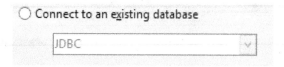

This option allows you to connect to a database in another application. It effectively makes LibreOffice Base a client of the other database. That's quite a complex concept so don't worry if you don't understand what it means – I'll explain it later on!

For this tutorial since we're creating a database from scratch the default option to create a new embedded database is perfectly fine. You can click on 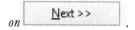 *.*

Registering the Database

You'll see a new page in the Database Wizard called **Decide how to proceed after saving the database**. This screen looks more intimidating than it is.

The first set of options deals with registering the database:

Do you want the wizard to register the database in LibreOffice?

⦿ Yes, register the database for me

○ No, do not register the database

When you register a database it allows LibreOffice to access (in other words use) the Database. So, in this case you definitely want to register the database automatically.

So, why wouldn't you want to register the database? Perhaps you are an advanced user and you want to set some of the options manually to increase performance.

In reality when making an embedded database you'll almost always go for the first option.

Opening the Database

The next option is fairly self-explanatory. Do you want to open the database for editing after it's been saved? I'd suggest that you do, so leave the check box ticked:

After the database file has been saved, what do you want to do?

☑ Open the database for editing

Editing the Database Tables with the Table editor

Next is the following text

box: ☐ Create tables using the table wizard .

Tables are quite an important concept in any database. They're the way that the computer stores information. While it's possible to create the tables without the table wizard it can simplify matters quite considerably if you use it.

So, for this tutorial I suggest that you check this box:

☑ Create tables using the table wizard

Java

Sometimes people start to experience problems with LibreOffice Base wizards if they don't have a recent version of Java installed. While your computer probably does already have Java installed if you experience problems with LibreOffice saying that Java is not installed properly while running any of the wizards or database features you can install Java manually by following the instructions at https://www.java.com/en/download/help/windows_manual_download.xml

Saving the Database

When you're happy with the options you've selected in the

Database wizard click on Finish . You'll see a save as dialogue. Change the location of the directory you're saving to and the name as appropriate. In this case I changed the file name to staff

File name: Staff .

When you're happy with your choices click on Save .

The Table Wizard

Now that you've created the database you'll see the main LibreOffice Base window. It's intimidating at first but we've chosen to create tables using the table wizard so that's what we'll concentrate on.

Our first view of the table wizard is the following:

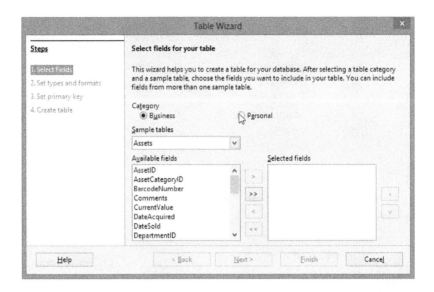

Because we're only creating an employee table, we want to remain in the business category

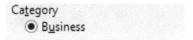

But we want to click on the Sample Tables:

And choose Employee from the list

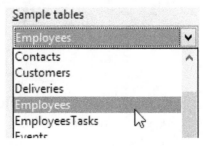

Note that when you've chosen a sample table the available fields change:

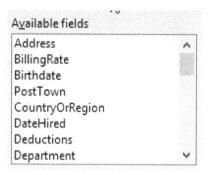

Earlier I said the database I was going to create would contain only:

- **Employee Number**
- **Staff name**
- **Telephone Number**
- **Address.**

So scroll down on the Available Fields list until you find the field that you want 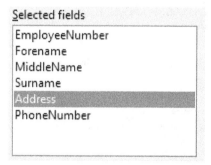 and double click on it.

Repeat the process until you've added all the fields that you want to add.

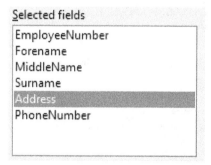

You can double click on any of the fields in the selected fields list to remove it from the list if you made a mistake when you added it.

Single click on any item in the list and then click on 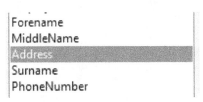 to move it up the list:

> Forename
> MiddleName
> Address
> Surname
> PhoneNumber

Or 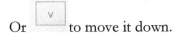 to move it down.

Set Types and Formats

Once you're happy with the fields you've added to your table click on Next > .

The Table Wizard allows you to set the format information for fields. This can include:

- Whether you have to enter the field
- Whether it's a number, text, picture or some other kind of data
- How large the field is (i.e. how many letters the field can contain if it's text.)

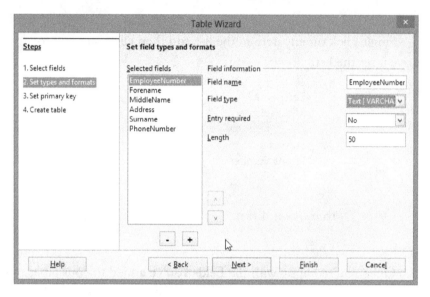

To change the format information for a field click on the field in the Selected Fields box. You'll see to the right of the field properties related to the field such as the field name, type, and entry required.

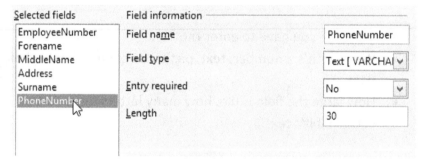

If you click on entry required and change it you can select whether LibreOffice will force you to have that field. Yes means that LibreOffice won't allow you to add a record without the field (i.e. you must have a phone number field to add an employee to the database), no means that the field isn't considered essential and you don't have to have it in order to add the data.

Note also the Length option. You can make a field longer or shorter using this. Obviously, you need to set the field length so it is as long as any item you'll add to the database. One thing to consider when you're setting the length is that it's always possible to increase the length of a field but if you reduce the length it may corrupt data. The longer a field is the more space LibreOffice will need to take up for each item in the list. This isn't normally that relevant for small databases but when you get a database with millions of items unnecessarily large fields can have a major impact on performance.

I've obviously left the type option in this dialogue to last because it scares a lot of people. But types are actually a fairly simple concept to understand. For example a field could be text – like the information you're reading now – or it could be a picture or a number.

Note, that Phone Number is a text field at the moment:

And I'm not going to change that!

A number will be a whole (negative or positive integer number) or a real number (a number with a decimal point) but it can't contain information like brackets, letters or symbols. So if you want to be able to include information like +044 (01892) 00000 you must use a text field.

But I will change the Employee Number field by clicking on it and changing it from text:

To Integer

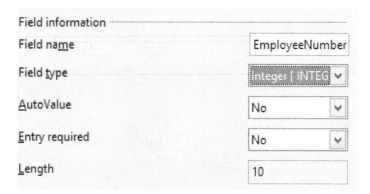

An integer is a whole number such as 1, -1, 53, 2222. It does not contain a decimal place.

Once I change the field to Integer, something else immediately changes. You have different formatting options:

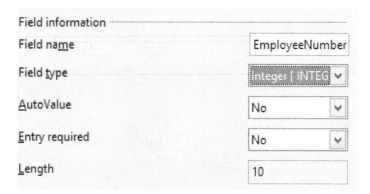

AutoValue is an interesting option. It means that LibreOffice will automatically provide a unique value to the field. It's used for primary keys (which I'll explain in a little while) where you want to make sure that you automatically generate a unique identifier.

In this case I'm changing the AutoValue to Yes:

You'll see a new option, the auto-increment statement option. This gives you the ability to change the way that LibreOffice automatically adds the value into the field. I'd suggest that you don't need to change this yet.

Auto-increment statement

When you're happy with your choices click on Next > .

Set Primary Key

Now we get some more jargon coming at us!

We've talked about databases being a collection of tables – which are information on a particular subject that's organised into fields. A Primary Key or Primary Field is a bit like a phone number. It's a field that is unique in the database which LibreOffice can use to look up a particular item in the table.

For example, every phone number is unique. Your telephone company will always know whose wires to send the message down when someone presses your phone number into their telephone.

Every Primary Key is unique. You can have a single field as a primary key, or a composite field (i.e. two or more fields in a table) but when combined they must result in a unique identifier.

In the Table Wizard we've now got a Primary Key field. At the moment it's set to create a Primary Key

☑ Create a primary key
  ⦿ Automatically add a primary key
  ☐ Auto value

But we've already got a field in our database table that looks like a primary key – the Employee Number. If the Number is unique then we can use it as a primary key without creating any new fields.

The ○ Use an existing field as a primary key option can be used when you think that you have already got a field that can act as a primary key. Click on it:

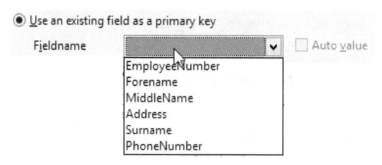

Then select EmployeeNumber in this case.

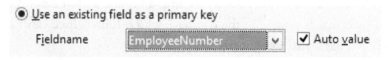

Notice that because we've already set EmployeeNumber to AutoValue that option is already checked. I'd advise almost always using the auto value option in a primary key.

There is a third option in the table wizard dialogue to use more than one field:

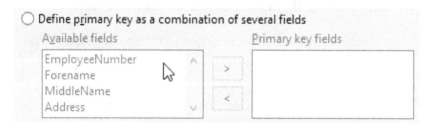

I'll explain that later on. It's most useful when you are making sure that a database runs as efficiently as possible, when making a database conform to third normal form (which sounds like a complete headache but it's really easy!)

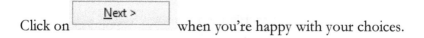 Click on when you're happy with your choices.

Creating the Table

The next screen you'll see in the table wizard allows you to create the table. First, change the name of the table if you want to:

Then chose what you want to do next – do you want to add data immediately, modify the table design manually, or create a Form?

I'm going to suggest that it's probably best at this stage to create a Form:

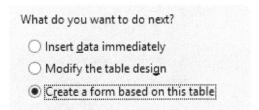

Since this will enhance the experience of your users when you come to add information to the database!

Click [Finish] to Finish the Table Wizard.

More Tables Please

A single database table isn't very flexible. We've created one table but it's possible to run the table wizard again and again. I'll explain how in a later chapter.

Next Chapter

In this chapter I've shown you how to create your first Database Table, an Employee Table.

In the next chapter I'm going to show you how to use the Form

Wizard to make forms that allow you to enter data into the database easily.

2 FORM WIZARD BASICS

In this chapter I'll show the basic use of the Form Wizard – making a form that makes it easier to add data to the database. In the last chapter you create an Employee Table, and populated it with fields. You also chose to run the Form Wizard after you'd created the table.

Field Selection

When the Form Wizard opens, it allows you to choose the fields that you want to use in the form. These can be from Tables or Queries. In this case you've just added one table, the Table called Employees so select that table.

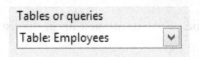

This will show a list of Available Fields

You can chose what fields to include in the form by double clicking on them. In this example I'd suggest that you click on all of them:

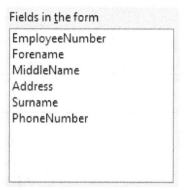

Then, if you want to change the order of a field click on it and then press either the ^ to move it up in the list or the v to move it down.

Click Next > when you are happy about what fields you've included in the form.

Set up a Sub form

This is a useful technique where you want to include information from other forms. For example, if you had a table on employees and a table on employee tasks you might use a sub form to show the tasks that an particular employee has as well as information on his name, address etc.

But, that's too complex for this stage of the book!

Leave the option unchecked: ☐ <u>A</u>dd Sub-form .

And click on Next > .

Arrange Controls

This page allows you to control how the form will be displayed on your screen. Note behind the wizard your choices have an impact on the actual form that you are designing so you'll be able to see the effect of them.

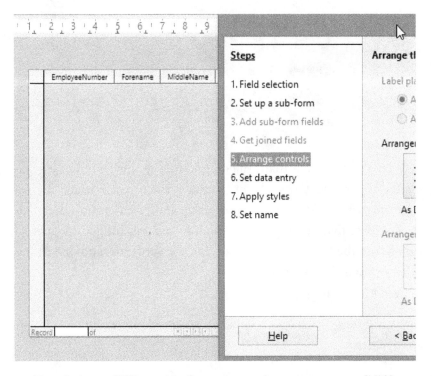

People have different preferences on the appearance of different forms. There's no "correct" decision here. LibreOffice sets the default as a data sheet – a sheet that looks almost like a spreadsheet. You can chose other arrangements below:

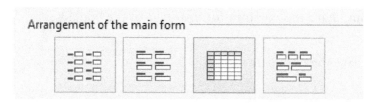

For example if you click on Columnar- Labels left the form will be displayed like so:

EmployeeNumt	
Forename	
MiddleName	
Surname	
Address	
PhoneNumber	

That's the option that I'm going to use on this form but it's all a matter of personal taste. The exception is when you're using subforms where I'd always suggest using a different arrangement for the subform than the main form (and, in general, I think it works best to use the "As Data Sheet" option for subforms and one of the other options for the main form).

Click on Next > when you're happy with the arrangement.

Set Data Entry

LibreOffice allows you to control whether you want to use a particular form to only enter new data

○ The form is to be used for entering new data only.
   Existing data will not be displayed

Or to also edit data:

⦿ The form is to display all data

If you chose to edit data, then you can also choose whether to allow the user to modify existing data

☐ Do not allow modification of existing data

Or to Delete a record

☐ Do not allow deletion of existing data

Or prevent a user from actually adding new data:

☐ Do not allow addition of new data

Selecting all three options will make a form that only displays data. In this case we are only going to be using the form to insert new data. We're not using it to modify existing data, so I select that option:

⦿ The form is to be used for entering new data only.
   Existing data will not be displayed

When you're happy with your selections click [Next >] .

Apply Styles

In the next page you can apply different colours (for example Light Grey) and difference data box appearance (for example, 3d).

When you chose an option on this list the form will change so you can see what it looks like.

Try out some, then click [Next >] when you're happy.

Set Name

You can chose the name of your form. I've changed the name to Insert Employees

Name of the form

| Insert Employees |

You can also choose whether to use the form (•) Work with the form or modify it once you've finished ( ) Modify the form . For this tutorial we're going to work with the form.

Click [Finish] when you're happy.

Some Thoughts

So far we've done pretty basic things with forms. But they are a very powerful component of LibreOffice allowing you to develop user interfaces that are both elegant and intelligent. I'm going to go into a lot more detail later on.

Using and Adapting the Form We Just Created

If you chose the Work with the Form option above during set name you'll see the form appear in your screen.

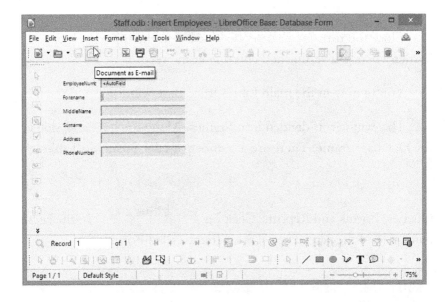

Note that EmployeeNumber should be an autofield. If you go to a field, type in the entry and press tab you'll be able to enter each field in turn.

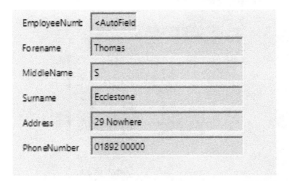

Note that when you reach the last field pressing tab will insert the next record

There's a problem with the form design, though. You can enter a number into EmployeeNumber. We want LibreOffice to automatically assign that rather than having someone enter it by hand.

Close the form by clicking on  at the top right hand corner when you've finished entering in the record.

You're now in the main LibreOffice Base window.

This window is divided into Frames. Along the left hand side is the Database frame. There are a number of tabs, including Tables, Queries, Forms and Reports. Click on . In the right hand side of the screen you'll see a frame called Forms.

Right click on the form you made earlier (Insert Employees) and then edit.

The window that you see is the form design window. It's quite a complicated window, although very powerful and useful. Note that at the top of the screen are menu options and task bars:

On the left hand are controls:

To the right hand side of the controls is the form that you created earlier using the Form Wizard:

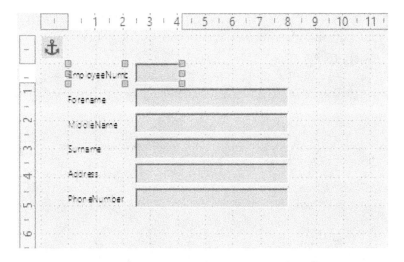

There's a lot to grasp here, but for this tutorial all we want to do is prevent the EmployeeNumber field from being editable by the end user. Right click on the field (i.e. the box)

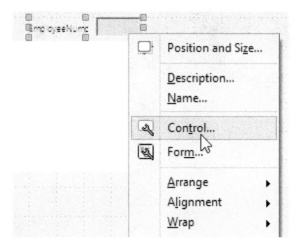

And then click on Control.

This allows you to edit some of the properties of the field (note, LibreOffice calls things like the text field you're editing a control. It also calls buttons, checkboxes, combo boxes and other similar features controls).

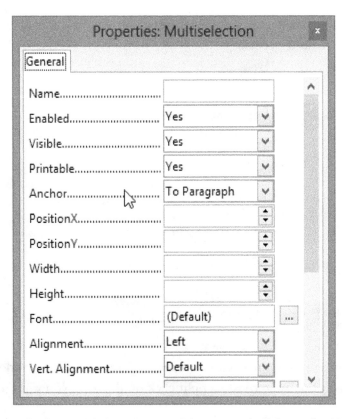

To edit the enabled property of the control click on the Yes

Select No:

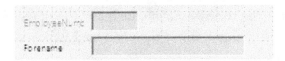

Click on [x] to close the dialogue. Note that the form has changes, greying out the Employee Number field:

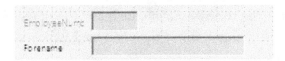

Save the form by clicking on 🖫 . Note that you can undo

changes you made using the Undo feature in the Edit menu. You can also use Redo if necessary.

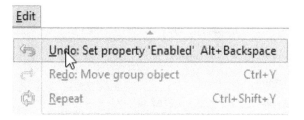

To close out of the Form Design Window click on Close in the File Menu.

If you've got any changes you haven't saved it will ask you if you want to save them. If you do, click Save .

Running a Form

Once more we're back to the main LibreOffice Base window. In the Forms dockable window right click on the form you want to run and then click on open.

Note that you're now running the Insert Employees form like before but this time you simply can't edit the EmployeeNumber field. It's protected.

You can add whatever information you want to the table via the form. Obviously, this is a very minor edit to the form. You can do a lot more in the Form Design window and I'll describe it later on.

Next Chapter

In this chapter I've described how to create a simple form to insert data. I've shown you a little bit of the Form Design window within LibreOffice. I've given you a tutorial on the Form Design Wizard. You've also seen the main LibreOffice Base window for the first time.

That's a lot of work!

In the next chapter I'm going to create a basic query. This allows you to get information out of the database that we're designing.

3 QUERY WIZARD BASICS

A query is a way of getting information out of your database. For example if you're creating an employee database and you want all employees with the surname Ecclestone you could run a query to get that information.

It's possible to create a query using SQL which is a programming language that most relational databases (for example, LibreOffice Base) supports. But that's a bit advanced for this stage of the book. Instead, we're going to create a query using a wizard that LibreOffice Base provides for the purpose.

Running the Query Wizard

In the main LibreOffice Base window go to the Database

dockable window and click on Queries . You'll see at the top right hand side of the screen a tasks dockable window. In it there is an option called Use Wizard to Create Query... . Click on it.

This will open up the Query Wizard on the Field Selection step.

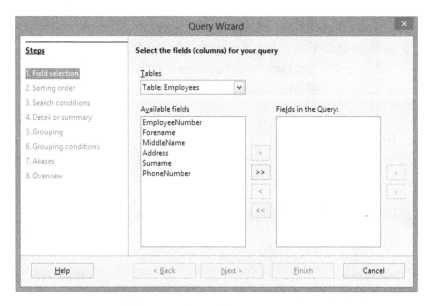

You can query using the fields in any table you've got in the database. Simply click on the Table name if you want to use a fields

from a different table. In this case we've just got one table in the database, so we're going to select fields from the table we have available.

Double click on the fields that you want in the query. You can have fields for three purposes:

1. Linking fields – fields that you use to join tables together. So, for example, if you need information from a table called Employee (Such as name, phone number) and another table called EmployeeTasks (such as projectID, duration) then an Employee Number field might link the two tables together. I'll explain this in more detail later on in the book.
2. Display fields – fields that you want to return as the result of your query and,

3. Condition fields – fields that you want to use to restrict the results of the query. For example, if the Employee table had salary and you wanted to restrict the result of the query to all employees who earn more than £10,000 you'd include the field.

If you change your mind about what fields you want to include in the query you can always use the < Back button.

I've just used included two fields in the query:

Fields in the Query:

Employees.Surname
Employees.PhoneNumber

When you're happy with the fields you've added, click Next > .

Sorting the Query results

LibreOffice uses a weird internal logic to return results – related to the order that items are entered into the database. Most people want to get the results of queries in an order that humans regard as logical. The next step in the query wizard allows you to sort the results.

Click on undefined to see the field that you want to sort the

results by

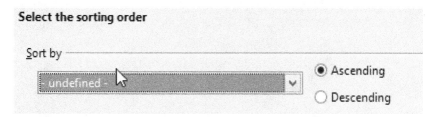

You'll see a list of fields you've included in the search. Select the first one that you want to sort by.

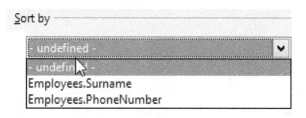

You can also choose whether you want to sort from A-Z (Ascending) or Z-A (Descending).

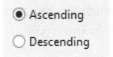

You can do then sort by another field. So, for example, if you have two employees with the same surname then you'd sort between those two items by whatever field is in the Then by box.

Might produce a sorted result like:

Alex 01892 333333

Ecclestone 0800 300000

Ecclestone 01892 00000

Farrow 07779 211111

When you're happy with your choices click 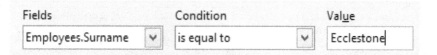.

Search Conditions

In the next screen you'll see conditions. These will allow you to select only data that you're interested in.

You can choose whether data has to match all of the conditions or only one of the conditions that you've chosen.

> ⦿ Match all of the following
> ◯ Match any of the following

One of the limits of the query wizard is that it only allows you to include static conditions. For example the condition:

Fields	Condition	Value
Employees.Surname ⌄	is equal to ⌄	Ecclestone

Would limit your search to people with employees that are identical to mine.

Note, though, that it is possible to create dynamic queries where you input the data to be searched. I'll show you how later on in the chapter.

When you're happy click 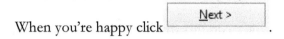 .

Note that we skip over some steps because we're only using data from one table.

Alias

The next screen allows you to set aliases for your fields. Often, because of programming conventions, field names can be particularly hard to decipher for end users. You can use Alias to make a field that might look be called kDbEmpNo into 'Employee Number' at least as far as the end customer is concerned.

Field	Alias
Employees.Surname	Surname
Employees.PhoneNumber	PhoneNumber

Note that whatever you type into the Alias box will be displayed in the query.

I changed it to:

Employees.Surname	Employee Surname

Overview

The next screen gives you an overview of the query that you've just made. The first step is to look at the name of the query field and change it to something that is more relevant.

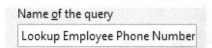

Name of the query

Lookup Employee Phone Number

There's something about the query that we've made so far that I don't like. I've created a static query – one that only displays items with a particular name. This can be useful for one off queries, but in general it's better to make queries that you can use all the time.

Now, it's not possible to do this within the query wizard. So, we're going to manually modify the query by checking ⦿ Modify Query .

Finally, check the overview to see if there is anything there that you want to change:

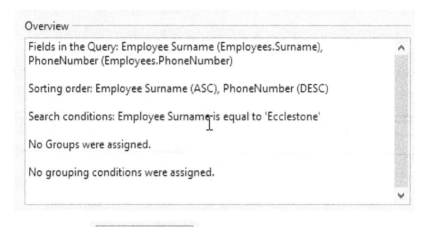

And click Finish .

This will open the Query Design Window. The Query Design Window, like the Form Design Window, gives you much more ability to change things than the wizard.

Making a Query Dynamic

We're now in the Query Design window. You can see a table with Field, Alias, Table, Sort, Visible, Function and Criterion.

Field	Surname	PhoneNumber
Alias	Employee Surna	PhoneNumber
Table	Employees	Employees
Sort	ascending	descending
Visible	☑	☑
Function		
Criterion	'Ecclestone'	

Some of these items are obvious from the query wizard. For example, we know what the Field means (i.e. we included Surname and PhoneNumber from the earlier query). Alias is how the field will be displayed.

The existence of the Table field is interesting. It's because in the case of joining two tables together you can have the same data in more than one table. For example, you might have Employee Number in the Employee table and also in the Project table.

Sort determines how we will sort the field, either ascending or descending.

Visible determines if we want to see the field. In this case, we don't really need to see Surname since that's the field that we're querying, so uncheck it.

Finally, Criterion. Notice that at the moment it's in single quotation marks 'Ecclestone' which means that it will match only Ecclestone. We're going to change it to a dynamic variable.

Field	Surname	PhoneNumber
Alias	Employee Surna	PhoneNumber
Table	Employees	Employees
Sort	ascending	descending
Visible	☐	☑
Function		
Criterion	:Surname	
Or		

This means that LibreOffice Base will prompt the user for that variable before comparing it to the result. Note that there are lots of different criterion we can use – for example we can use larger than, less than, like, equal to, not equal to and so on. We'll explain that later on.

Here's another thing to note. At the moment we're running a query on a text field. LibreOffice distinguishes by default between text that is upper case and text that is lower case. So, it doesn't consider Ecclestone and ecclestone to be the same text.

We can fix this problem (if, indeed, it is a problem) in table design by controlling what types we give an object.

Running the query

To run the query from the Query Design Window click on ⬛↓ Run Query   F5 in the edit menu.

LibreOffice will ask you what value you want for surname. Enter in the value

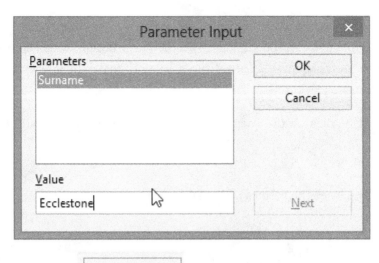

Then click 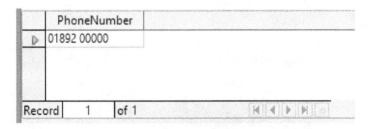.

You'll see the result of the query in the top dockable window.

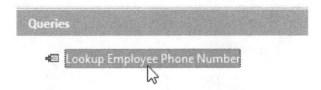

	PhoneNumber	
▷	01892 00000	

Record   1   of 1 |◀ ◀ ▶ ▶|

Save the changes to the query by clicking on 💾 then close out of the query using the ✕ Close in the file menu.

Note that when you're in the main LibreOffice Base window you can run the query by double clicking it in the query dockable window:

Queries

◀▤ Lookup Employee Phone Number

Making a Query into a Form

While you can run a query from the query design window, most people prefer to make a form from a query to make the interface much more elegant.

Right click on the query in the Query dockable window and then click on 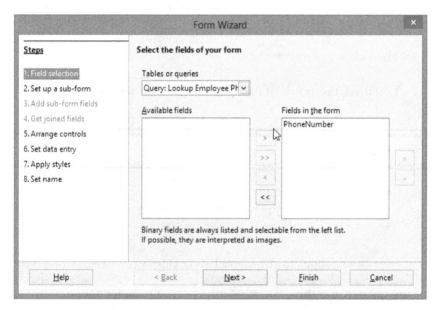 Form Wizard... .

You'll see the form wizard dialogue that we saw in the last chapter:

You go through the same process, adding the fields you want in the form then clicking Next > .

You don't want a sub-form in this case so leave the box unchecked ☐ Add Sub-form and click Next > .

I prefer to leave reports as datasheets, so click Next > .

In the next screen you're left with a choice on whether to allow the user to update the data.

- ⦿ The form is to display all data
  - ☐ Do not allow modification of existing data
  - ☐ Do not allow deletion of existing data
  - ☐ Do not allow addition of new data

This depends on what you want the form to do. For example you might want a form that allows you to update a particular record in which case you'd leave the boxes unchecked. Alternatively, you might simply want a query form.

I'm going to allow you to change the data in this form so I click Next > but it's really dependent on what you want the form to do.

The next screen allows you to change the appearance of the form. Choose the layout that you want, then click Next > .

Finally, change the name of the form if you want to:

Name of the form

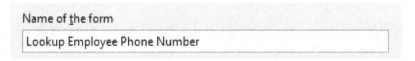

Lookup Employee Phone Number

And obviously decide whether to use the form or change it. I'm just going to use the form.

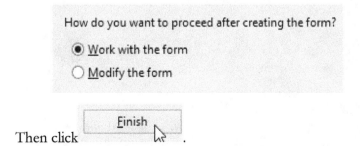

How do you want to proceed after creating the form?

- ⦿ Work with the form
- ○ Modify the form

Then click Finish .

Note that when the form runs because it is a dynamic query LibreOffice will ask for the variable that we used. Type in the value you want then click OK

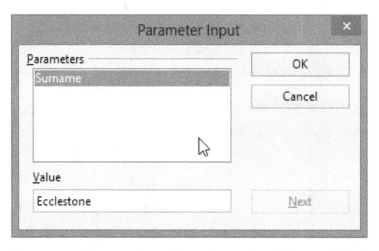

The query will run and you'll see the result of the query in the Form window:

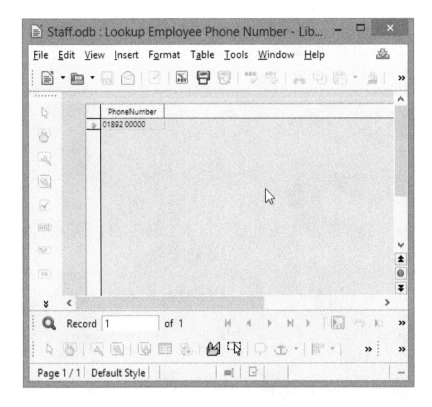

Note that you can edit the form in the Form Design window as normal.

Next Chapter

In this chapter I've described how to run basic queries, including a dynamic query. I've also shown you how to make a form from the result of a query.

In the next chapter I'm going to go into more information about database design. In particular, we're going to extend the database so that it has several tables.

4 DATABASES WITH MORE THAN ONE TABLE.

So far we've worked with a very simple database. It's allowed us to see the main parts of LibreOffice – Forms, Queries and Tables. But it's just not a very powerful database. Most databases rely on more than one Table.

This is where databases become a little trickier to understand since you need to know how to design the database into separate tables and how to combine them together again when you need information from more than one table.

Why do you need more than one Table?

So far we've worked with a table that's called employee. It contains only information about Employees such as surname, phone number etc. That's perfectly good – as long as you only want to store information about employees.

But suppose you want to store information about their expenses?

I guess in theory you could add fields that relate to expenses into the employee chart. But a single employee can have dozens or hundreds of expenses. Adding a field for each expense just isn't going to work. And expenses are related to projects, and customers, and so on.

Adding data to a single table would start to be impossible.

What you need are tables that are related to different subjects. So, you need a table for Expenses, and a table for Employee, and a table for Projects, and a table for customers etc…

Dividing a Database into Tables

This book is mainly about using LibreOffice Base rather than the rather complex issues involved in database design. When designing a database you need to think about what you're going to store. You can think of a table as a subject area – so, Surname, Phone Number etc. are fields in a database that are all related to employees. Project budget, project objective, project deadline are all related to projects. Task, ProjectID, Task description is all related to tasks.

Some fields may belong in more than one database table. That's generally the case if you have a key field – such as EmployeeID, ProjectID etc.

When designing a database one of the primary concerns is that all data except keys should only be stored in one place. So, if you have an Employee with a surname you only store the surname in the employee table.

If, say, you want to report the surname of the project manager in the project table you link the two fields (Employee and Project) using keys, and then do a join when running queries.

The reason for this is that when you duplicate data you create a database that is very susceptible to errors.

Because there is a lot to learn and this is a book dedicated mainly to using a particular software program rather than database design I'm afraid that the discussion in this section may not be particularly clear. I could write an entire book on database design but fortunately someone else already has and it's rather good. I recommend getting your hands on Database Design for Mere Mortals: A Hands-On Guide to Relational Database Design by Michael J. Hernandez.

Using Table Design View

Once you've designed your database you can create the tables from the table design window. In the Database dockable window

click on Tables then in the tasks dockable window click on ▢ Create Table in Design View... .

The Tables Design View will open:

	Field Name	Field Type	
▷			

Each row corresponds to a field. First type a name in the Field Name column. Note that by default the Field Type is TEXT.

	Field Name	Field Type
▷	TaskID	Text [VARCHAR]

A VARCHAR type allows you to type text, but it's important to note that LibreOffice considers upper case and lower case to be different in the even that you're doing a condition when you use the VARCHAR type.

You can describe a field by entering text into the Description box.

	Field Name	Field Type	Description
▷	TaskID	Text [VARCHAR]	This field will be the primary key

Right click on the green triangle to allow you to cut, copy or delete the row. You can also insert a new row if you want to add a field in between to existing fields. One limitation of the design view is that you can't easily move a field up or down in the table order once you've created any data in the table.

Note that you can also make a field a Primary Key.

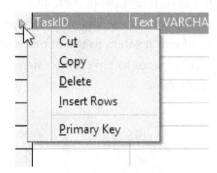

Clicking in the Field Type column allows you to set a type:

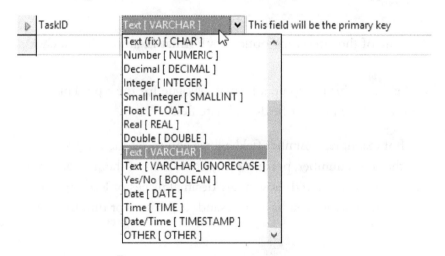

I'll describe what these types mean in a little while.

Field Properties

When we were using the Table Wizard earlier we set a number of properties. When you are in a row in the table design view you can also set field properties.

Each data type has different properties, although Length (in the case of numbers this relates to how large the number you can store in the field, in the case of text it refers to the number of letters you can store), whether you're required to have something in the field (Entry required), and a default value.

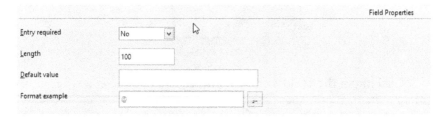

One of the interesting options is Format Example. If you click on the [image] this brings up a format dialogue for the type. This is most useful for number fields and date fields.

For example, a number field allows you to set the category (whether it's a number, percent etc.), the format of the number (how the number is displayed) how many decimal places or leading zeroes to use, and whether you have thousands separators or turn the field red if negative.

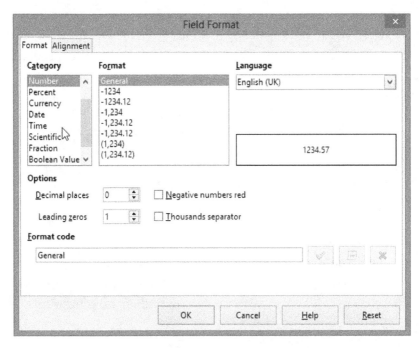

Formatting options change depending on what kind of field you are creating but they are generally self-explanatory.

Clicking on the Alignment tab allows you to control the horizontal alignment of the field.

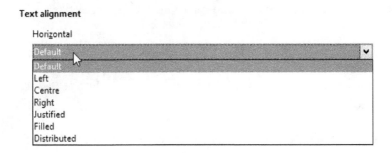

Again, there are often slightly different options depending on the field type but the options are self-explanatory.

Data Types

When you're creating a new field in the Table Design View you are given the option of choosing a data type. I've already explained a little bit about this. All data has a type. If you try to enter data that doesn't conform to the type LibreOffice will prevent you doing so.

LibreOffice uses most of the standard SQL Types:

Integer Types

An integer is a whole number (i.e. -1, 2, 5 etc.) without and decimal places. So, 55 is a whole number and 55.32 isn't.

One of the things that can confuse a nonprogrammer is that you have multiple different types of integers. These relate to the amount of storage that the database assigns to the field. So, for example, a Tiny Integer [TINYINT] takes up less space than a Big Integer [BIGINT].

The problem comes when your integer type is too small for the data that you want to store. If this happens you can get overflow errors that corrupt the information you are storing in the database.

Therefore, I generally suggest either using Integer or Big Integer rather than the smaller data types unless you are making a huge database that will come close to the capabilities of LibreOffice.

NOTE: these definitions can vary between database platforms. While we are using the embedded database for LibreOffice at this point in the book you will need to make sure that you familiarise yourself with the exact definition that your database uses.

Tiny Integer [TINYINT] – Accepts integers with a fixed length of three spaces.

Small Integer [SMALLINT] – Accepts integers with a fixed length of five spaces.

Integer [INTEGER] – Accepts integers with a fixed length of ten spaces. You can also set an autovalue field.

Big Integer [BIGINT] – Accepts integers with a fixed length of nineteen spaces.

Note that although I consider some other types such as real and floating point to be fractional number types you can often use them as integer types as well.

Real Number Types

A real number is a number that contains a decimal place, such as 1.24 or -12.2. Again, there are multiple data types of different sizes so that you can optimise the database if necessary.

Number [NUMERIC] – Can be set to handle whole numbers, numbers with decimals and also fractions.

Decimal [DECIMAL] – Primarily used to handle numbers with decimal points. You can set the number of decimal places.

Float [FLOAT] – Floating point numbers are numbers with decimal places that are up to 17 spaces long. It's compatible with most other database applications.

Real [REAL] – Similar to Float, but it can handle numbers with more than 17 spaces long.

Double [DOUBLE] – theoretically contains double the amount of storage of float. Similar to Real. Used to be compatible with other database applications.

Other Number Types

Binary numbers are fundamental to computing. LibreOffice provides two binary types for your convenience.

Binary [VARBINARY] – On the face of it used to handle binary code. But there is a large range of applications you can use with a binary storage area… almost all files are ultimately stored as Binary code, as are images and etc.

Binary (fix) [BINARY] – Similar to Binary [VARBINARY] but you can specify how large a number of spaces the field contain s.

Text Types

You're reading text now – it's a combination of letters, numbers and punctuation marks. LibreOffice has several text types that can be very useful when you are creating a new database.

Memo [LONGVARCHAR] – Used for very long texts. Can theoretically accept entries of up to 2 billion spaces.

Text (fix) [CHAR] – Text field where you can set a specific number of characters. Useful for things like number plates where you know exactly what will be in the field.

Text [VARCHAR]- The default field which can accept text (letters, numbers, special characters) of all types. Considers lower and upper case letters to be different values.

Text [VARCHAR_IGNORCASE] – Similar to Text [VARCHAR] but considers upper and lower case to be the same number.

Other Types

Sometimes you want to record a true or false answer (a Boolean answer), include an image or date or time in your database. LibreOffice allows you to do this with some other more specialist data types.

Image [LONGVARBINARY] – Designed to support image files. Depends on the particular implementation of the database that you are using.

Yes/No [BOOLEAN] – Supports binary code, i.e. true or false values.

Date [DATE] – You can accept a date in a format that you choose.

Time [TIME] – You can accept a time in a format you choose.

Date / Time [DATETIME] – You can accept a date and time.

Other [OTHER] – A general field that you can put anything into. No validation.

Delete a field

To delete a field right click on the square to the left of the field in the Table Design View:

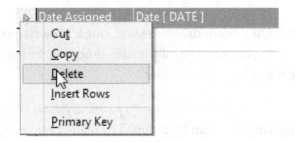

This will highlight the field, and give you a list of options about what to do with the field. Click on Delete.

Note that if you Delete a field you will lose the data in it!

Data Validation

In some very expensive database systems it's possible to create data validation rules that automatically check data when you put it into the database. While LibreOffice does this to an extent with primary keys, the method it uses isn't as sophisticated as other database systems I have seen.

Therefore, you will need to include some basic validation in database forms.

Entity Relationships

Some computer scientists decided that a posh way of naming tables was to call them Entities. The first main question when you're making a database is what tables you need but then the second is what relationships they should have.

You can think of relationships as links between related tables. For example, and project may have a project manager who is an employee of the company. There's a relationship between the project and the employee table.

These relationships take three forms: *a one to one relationship…* for example an employee may have a single bank account that the company makes a payment to, and each bank account can only be related to one employee. Or an employee can have a single office assigned to him, and each private office can only be assigned to an employee.

In general, if a relationship is one to one it's always possible to merge the tables, but conceptually it can sometimes be better to keep one-to-one related entities separate.

A *One to Many* relationship is a very typical relationship. For example, one employee can be assigned to many projects. Or one project can have many tasks.

In fact, there's a concept called third normal form that tries to resolve all many-to-many relationships into one-to-many. You do this by creating a linking table with a composite key.

So, if we have many employees can be assigned to many projects, we'd create a table called Assigned to Project which links the two:

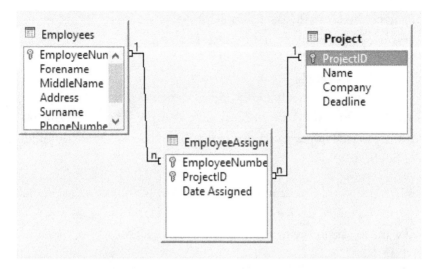

That may be a strange concept to some people but note that in the above diagram we've added information that doesn't really belong in either the employees or the project table. By designing a database that is normalised from the start - i.e. one where you break down many-to-many relationships and only data in one table in the database rather than in multiple places – it is much easier to extend and change the database as the system grows.

Again, because I've only skimmed the surface you may be confused right now. I'd suggest getting a book on relational database design if you're going to develop complex databases.

WARNING: Fields used in multiple tables

Where you are using the same fields in multiple tables it is very important that the definition of the field is the same in both tables. This includes data type, length, whether it is required etc.

Data types that are different won't link and will introduce a lot of errors into the database.

As a general rule if your database is correctly designed you will only have the same field in multiple places when it is a key, i.e. one that is used to identify an item in the database.

Composite Keys

A key must always be unique. But sometimes, when you're normalising your database to break up a many-to-many relationship the most logical key is a composite key. That is, a key that combines two fields.

It's pretty easy to create a composite key in the table design view. First, in the tables dockable window right click on the table where you want to assign the primary key and click edit.

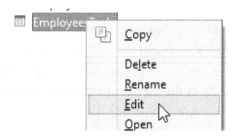

This will open the table design window.

Click on the square to the left of the first row containing a field you want to be a primary key. This will highlight the row.

	Field Name	Field Type	
	EmployeeNumber	Integer [INTEGER]	
	TaskID	Integer [INTEGER]	

Press shift, and click on the square for the next field you want to be a primary key.

Field Name	Field Type
EmployeeNumber	Integer [INTEGER]
TaskID	Integer [INTEGER]

Repeat until you've highlighted all the rows. Then right click on the triangle.

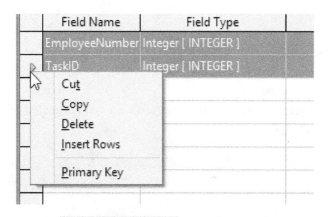

And click on _____ Primary Key _____. Note that the key icon will appear by the primary keys you've just inserted.

Field Name	Field Type
EmployeeNumber	Integer [INTEGER]
TaskID	Integer [INTEGER]

You can then click off onto an empty square, and press 💾 to save the form and ✕ Close in the file menu to close it.

Implementing Relationships

So far we've designed the database and created it. Now we have to create the relationships between tables.

59

In the main LibreOffice Window click on Tables in the Database Dockable window.

You'll see the list of tables that you've already created in the Tables Dockable Window:

Tables

⊞ EmployeeAssignedProject
⊞ Employees
⊞ EmployeesTasks
⊞ Project
⊞ Tasks

In the Tools menu click on Relationships..↖.

If there are any tables that aren't included in your Relationship Manager you'll see the Add Tables dialogue.

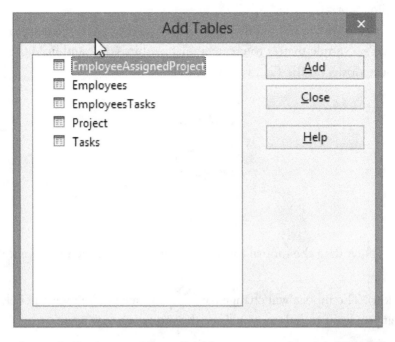

As a rule I suggest adding all tables you want by simply double clicking on them, then clicking on 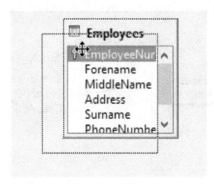 .

Note that when you add a table, it won't necessarily be in the position that you want in the Relationships View. Click and hold on the title of the table then drag it to wherever you want. While you're dragging it you'll see a ghost image and the mouse will change to a cross:

Adding a relationship

Once you've moved the tables about so they're convenient to you it's a simple matter to create a relationship. Click and hold the mouse down on the field you want to link.

Then drag the mouse towards the other table which you want to link to. The mouse will change to ⊘ . Once you're over the field that you want to link to, you'll see the mouse change again.

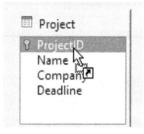

Let go of the mouse.

All being well, you'll see the new link either the new link:

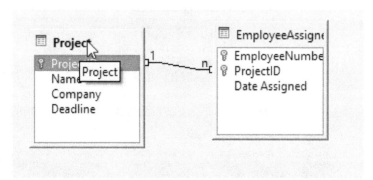

Or the Relations dialogue that you saw earlier.

Sometimes, you may see a warning dialogue which means that you can't link the field because they are of different types:

Also, you need to remember to be very careful about the fields you link. It's possible that a field can have the same type as your primary key in which case you could theoretically link the two fields together. This would result in an awful mess at a later stage of your database. So, be careful!

The Relationship Dialogue

You use the Relationship Dialogue to control what happens when you update or delete a record in one table which references or is referenced by another table. You can choose for it to have no effect, or for it to automatically update related items in other tables.

Sometimes the relationship Dialogue is opened immediately on creating a link but you can always open it yourself by double clicking on a link where you want to change Relationship Properties:

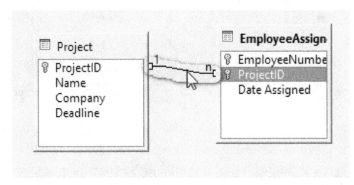

This will bring up the Relationship dialogue. The first two sections allow you to see the table involved, and the fields involved. You can change the fields by clicking on them, although I generally suggest that you do this through the GUI rather than the Relationships dialogue.

The next section contains the *Update Options*.

By default, these are set to No action which means that when you change a primary key it doesn't have any effect on the data in any other table.

Update Cascade Will update all corresponding key fields in other tables if a primary key is updated.

Set Null If the Primary Key has been modified all corresponding external keys are set to null.

Set Default If the Primary Key has been modified all corresponding external keys are set to a default value that you specify.

Delete Options work the same way as Update Options, but they are only activated when you delete an item in a table rather than when you update it. Click [OK] to save your relationship properties, and don't forget to click 💾 to save any changes you make.

Queries in multiple table databases

When working with multiple tables it's generally best to work in the Query Design View and the Form Design View rather than using the wizards. This is because the Wizards are less powerful and tend to make mistakes like failing to take into account the joins between the database tables.

We've already seen the use of the Query Design View when we were trying to make a query dynamic.

Fortunately, the addition of multiple tables doesn't really complicate matters very much.

Opening the Query Design View

Queries

In the main LibreOffice Base window click on   .

The Tasks dockable window has an option called Create Query in Design View... . Click on it.

You'll see the Add Table or Query dialogue. Click on the tables that contain the information that you need.

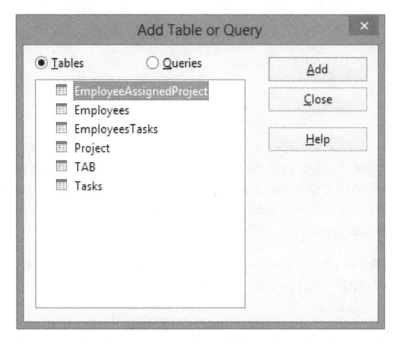

For example, if you want to display a list of employees and the projects they are assigned to you'll need Employees, EmployeeAssignedProject, and Project.

Note that middle one. Where you have a many to many relationship you often break it down by having an "intermediate" or linking table. Where the link between two tables isn't direct you'll need to include these intermediate tables.

You won't necessarily show them in the final query, but it's necessary to include them at this stage.

When you've added the tables you want, click [Close]. Note that if you make a mistake and need to change the tables you'll be able to in the main query design view.

Writing the query

We're now in the main Query Design View.

Note that in the top of the query Design View is a pane showing the tables that you're using to create the query. You can also see the relationships between those tables.

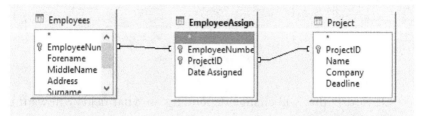

We've seen the bottom pane before, which produces the query. In this case we want to show the employee number and surname, the Project ID, Name and Deadline:

So, first double click on EmployeeNumber on the Employee Table

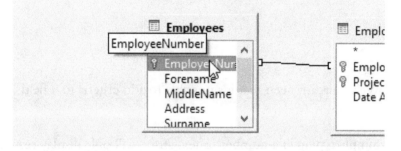

You'll see that in the bottom pane the field is added:

Field	EmployeeNumb		
Alias			
Table	Employees		
Sort			
Visible	☑	☐	☐
Function			

Keep on adding the other fields by double clicking on them until you've inserted all the items that you need.

Field	EmployeeNumb	Surname	ProjectID	Name	Deadline
Alias					
Table	Employees	Employees	Project	Project	Project
Sort					
Visible	✔	✔	✔	✔	✔
Function					

Obviously that will change depending on what fields you want to include in the query.

If you were to run the query as it stands you'd get a list of all the employees' assigned projects:

	EmployeeNumber	Surname	ProjectID	Name	Deadline
▷ 1		Ecclestone	1	Project 1	

Adding Criteria to the Query

We've already seen that it's possible to add criteria to a field using the criteria square.

Simply typing in a number or text string will only display results were a record is equal to that static value.

There are other operators, such as

< less than

<= less than or equal to

> greater than

>= greater than or equal to

LIKE – an operator for strings that means it will search for items that are similar to the item, i.e. it resolves regular expressions.

You can combine these operations with a variable, so:

Field	EmployeeNumb
Alias	
Table	Employees
Sort	ascending
Visible	✔
Function	
Criterion	< :maxno
Or	

Will match with all employees less than a variable that you request.

You can join criterion together using AND if necessary. For example, this | Criterion | < :maxno AND > 5 | will change the criteria so that it matches only those employeenumbers that are both less than the variable maxno but also greater than 5.

Note the OR sections under criteria. AND requires both values to be correct for the criteria to be correct, OR allows either value to be correct for the record to be displayed.

Criterion	< :maxno
Or	>5

Means that if an Employee number is less than maxno it will be displayed. It will also be displayed if it is greater than 5. So, if you chose a maxno of 3, employees 1, 2, 6, 7... infinity (i.e. not 3, 4, 5) will be displayed.

That's a reasonably difficult concept to explain, but think of these two statements:

I'll go to the bus stop if it's not raining and I have time.

I'll go to the bus stop if it's not raining or I don't have access to a car.

They mean subtly different things.

Note that there are a number of other operators that you can use. I've given you a basic list, but you can get the full list from the LibreOffice help.

Sorting a field

If you want to sort a field simply go to the Sort row, double click on the empty square that belongs to the field and choose whether to sort it in ascending or descending order.

Field	EmployeeNumb
Alias	
Table	Employees
Sort	(not sorted) ⌄
Visible	(not sorted)
	ascending
Function	descending
Criterion	

Hiding a Field

Sometimes you only want to use a field for 'administrative' purposes, for example you might want to sort results by the field or put a criteria on query based on that field but not show it.

It's easy to hide a field. Simply go to the visible checkbox and disable it by clicking on the square. In the following example I've just hidden the Surname field:

Field	EmployeeNumb	Surname	ProjectID	Name	Deadline
Alias					
Table	Employees	Employees	Project	Project	Project
Sort					
Visible	☑	☐	☑	☑	☑
Function					

You can show a field again by going to the square and clicking it so it shows a tick.

Functions

A function allows LibreOffice to do various things like display the Maximum value in a set of returned results, count the number of returned results, or give you the average. Double click on the Functions box to see a list of the functions available for LibreOffice Base:

```
(no function)
Average
Count
Maximum
Minimum
Sum
Every
Any
Some
STDDEV_POP
STDDEV_SAMP
VAR_SAMP
VAR_POP
Collect
Fusion
Intersection
Group
```

Say you want to produce the number of projects a particular Employee is assigned to. You'd use something like the following

Field	EmployeeNumb	ProjectID
Alias		Number Of Proj
Table	EmployeeAssign	EmployeeAssign
Sort	ascending	
Visible	☑	☑
Function	Group	Count

Count as a function is obvious: it simply counts the number of items of a particular type. The Group function is a bit like a sort. It makes LibreOffice clump all identical employee numbers together in the results.

You can find out more about functions in the LibreOffice help.

Running the query

You can run the query by clicking on 🔂 Run Query   F5 in the edit menu. You'll see a preview of the query results:

EmployeeNumber	ProjectID	Date Assigned	Name	Deadline
1	1	25/04/14	Project 1	

You can turn the preview off by clicking on ✔ Preview   F4 in the View menu.

Showing the SQL of a Query

This is a function for an advanced user, but if you understand SQL it can be very useful to see what code the Query Design View is generating.

Click on  in the view menu to see the SQL:

```
SELECT "Employees"."EmployeeNumber", "EmployeeAssignedProject"."ProjectID",
       "EmployeeAssignedProject"."Date Assigned", "Project"."Name", "Project"."Deadline"
FROM   "EmployeeAssignedProject", "Employees", "Project"
WHERE  "EmployeeAssignedProject"."EmployeeNumber" = "Employees"."EmployeeNumber"
       AND "EmployeeAssignedProject"."ProjectID" = "Project"."ProjectID"
ORDER BY "Employees"."EmployeeNumber" ASC
```

(Note, firstly, that the code you see will be different to the above since I've added some white space to make it easier to read. Also, you'll find that you can also alter the SQL manually using this view. There are things that a GUI just can't handle as well as direct coding but that's a very advanced subject!)

Next Chapter

We've covered a huge amount of ground in this chapter. I've shown you how to implement multiple tables, control the relationship between tables, and also how to query them.

In the next chapter we're going to go back to the form design since we've only created forms that reference a single table so far.

5 FORM DESIGN FOR MULTIPLE-TABLE DATABASES

When you start to work with multiple-table databases the form design becomes a little bit more complex. While you can create forms for individual tables, what happens when you get a linking table? Or where you need to show data from more than one Table?

This chapter will seek to answer those questions.

I'll describe how to use Database Views, but I'll also describe how to use subforms in the Form Design Wizard.

Views

We've dealt with Tables, Queries and Forms so far. Views are the fourth major element of a relational database – but the good thing is that they're very similar to tables from the point of view of an end user. Essentially, Tables are how the database is organised, but sometimes this organisation doesn't match how you "think" or a database.

A view is dynamically generated by LibreOffice from the information in the database tables, and allows you to manipulate data the way that you want to.

To create a view click on Tables in the database dockable window then 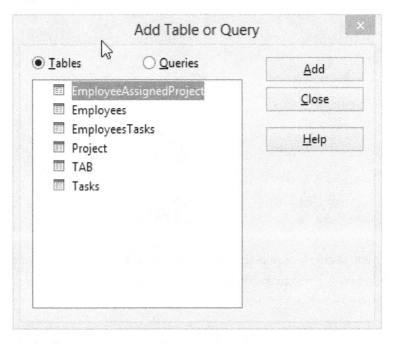 Create View... in tasks.

You'll see an Add Table or Query dialogue which you can use in the same way you would in the Table Design view

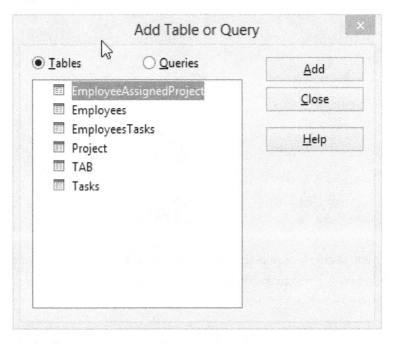

Double click on the Tables you want (Employees, EmployeesTask, and Tasks in this case)

The View Design window works exactly the same as the Query Design window. You can add fields by double clicking on them, sort, set criteria and even use functions although I don't think that is recommended.

When you want to create a report that displays information aggregated from a number of tables creating a view first can be a useful step to simplify matters.

You can create a report or a form from a view by right clicking on it from the Tables dockable window and using the Form or Report wizard in the same way you'd make a form from a normal Table.

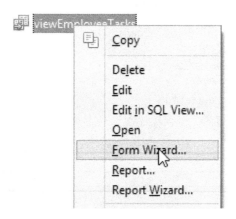

One thing to note is that you won't be able to edit the data in a form or report you make from a view. You need to use another method to do that.

Sub-forms

When you've created a table that references other forms you can use a subform. It allows you to display related information.

In the Tables dockable window right click and select Form Wizard as normal

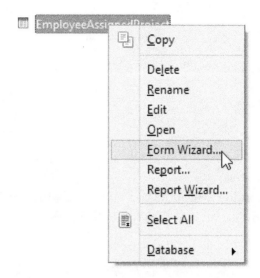

Follow the first step as normal, clicking on the fields that you want to include:

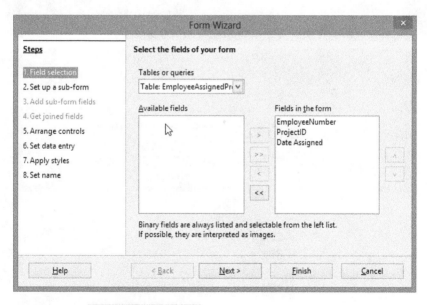

Click on [Next >]

Set up a sub-form

In the next step click on 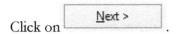. You'll want to leave the selection of fields as ⦿ Sub-form based on manual selection of fields

.

Click on [Next >] .

Add Sub-Form fields

The next window will allow you to choose what sub-form fields you want to add. Just double click on the fields that you want to show.

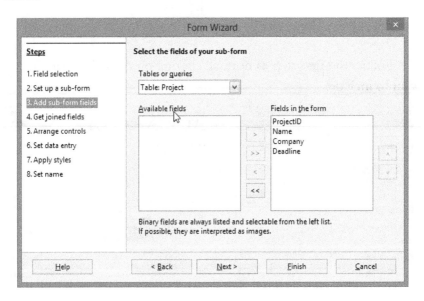

Click on [Next >] .

Get Joined Fields

This next step looks complicated, but actually it's fairly simple.

Just use the table design you created as a guide. Your main table might be EmployeeAssignedTask and your subform might be from Task. In that case, the key that links the tables might be TaskID.

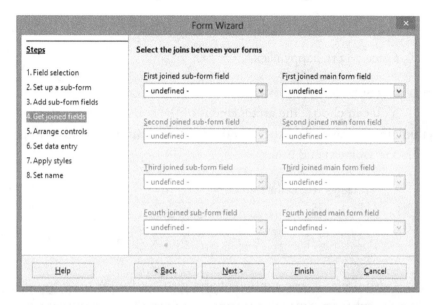

Once you know that the link is based on TaskID, you join them based on that knowledge. Simply put in the key field for the subform, and the key field for the main form field.

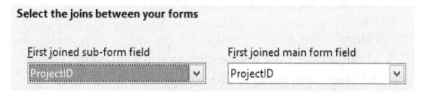

If there are more than one linking fields for the subform, include each. The order is important from a database efficiency point of view, since anything rejected by the first join won't be included in subsequent joins. BUT, in practice this only matters if you're doing a very large database.

Once you're happy click 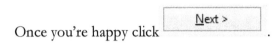 .

Arrange Sub-form

You can choose the arrangement of the subform. As a rule, I think that using as data sheet tends to be best. But it depends on your personal opinion and taste.

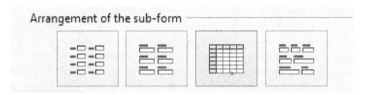

I also prefer to use a different arrangement for the main form than the subform. Since this is a matter of taste I'd suggest that you experiment and see what you like.

Once you're happy click .

Further steps

You can choose what update options you want, what style you want, and what name to call it. These steps have already been explained earlier so I won't detail them here.

When you open the form you might see something like this:

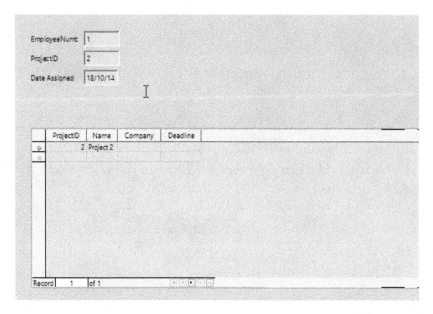

Note, though that there are certain limitations in the Form Design Wizard. When you are creating a form that is used to update a table you might want to actually design the form yourself using the Form Design View.

Form Design View

If you want to control the GUI of a database the Form Design view is one of the most powerful features of LibreOffice. And, because it is so powerful, it's no surprise that it can take some learning.

Rather than trying to go straight off into the Form Design view for a blank form I'm going to use a form that we've already created with the LibreOffice Base Form Wizard. While this has certain disadvantages – because the Form Wizard only gives you a very basic level of control – it means that we won't have to do everything from scratch.

As you become more advanced at LibreOffice Base you'll be able to do a heck of a lot from this view. But as a beginners book I'm going to try to stop this from becoming too scary.

Opening a form in Design View

To open an existing Form in the Form Design View go to the

Forms

Forms dockable window by clicking on   in the Database dockable window. Then right click on the form you want to open and click on edit:

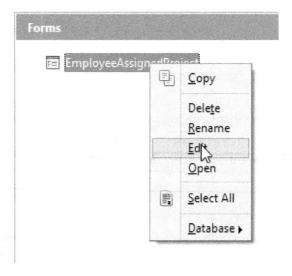

You'll see the form open up.

The Form Design View probably looks scary at first. There's a heck of a lot going on.

Main Window

The Form Design View is divided into several parts. The first part that you will probably notice is the main working window, which is bounded by rulers – in the same way a LibreOffice writer window is bounded. This contains the CONTROLS and LABELS of the form.

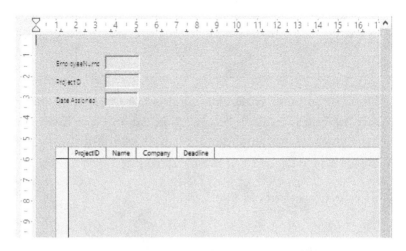

What is a control? A control is something like a text field, a picture, a button. Something that is active in the form allowing you to display or change data. For example  is a control called a text box. You enter or display text in it.

What is a label? A label is a piece of static text that informs you what a control does. For example Emp oyeeNume is a label.

Control Dockable Window

To the left of the main editing area you can see a list of controls

Each of these allow you to do something. For example allows you to select and move a control or label. Allows you to put a push button onto the form.

Using a computer system like windows or Linux you'll have regularly used these controls before. Although this may be the first time you've seen something meant to add them to the form you'll intuitively know what most of these controls do.

They're not as scary as they look!

Menu Bar

This probably needs no introduction because you'll have seen it before in a lot of applications!

File   Edit   View   Insert   Format   Table   Tools   Window   Help

You use it to do things like save, change alignment, and insert controls.

Task Bar

Again, this isn't rocket science. You'll use it to do things like save, highlight, and change the font of labels.

Property Dockable window

On the right hand side of the main editing area you can see a list of properties.

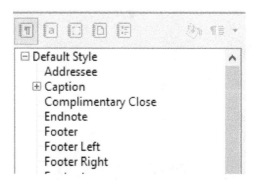

This allows you to change the appearance of controls and labels

Removing a control from the form

To remove a control from the form simply click on it to select it (you'll see green squares around it)

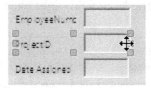

And then press backspace, delete or del on the keyboard.

Adding a label to a form

A label is the first control that most people use. Click on ABC in the list of controls. Then go to the place on the form that you want to insert the label and draw a box where you want the label to be (click and hold the mouse down, then move the mouse to the opposite corner of the rectangle):

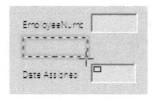

Let go.

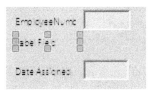

You've added a new label but it's not particularly good yet!

Changing the text in a label field

Obviously, at the moment the label is just a default placeholder. You'll need to change some things about it before it's any use to you. To change the text of the label field, right click on the field and then click on control.

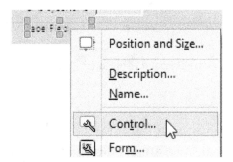

We've seen the following properties dialogue before when we wanted to make a field disabled. Now that we're designing something that is more complex we're going to use more of the functionality.

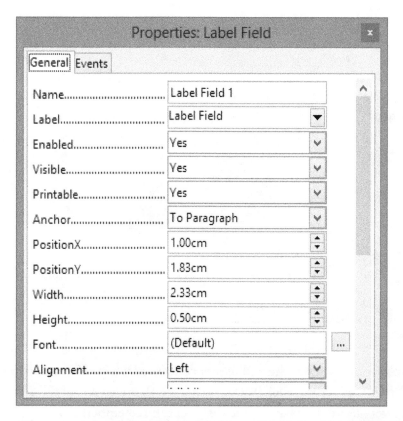

The properties dialogue is divided into General – which we will use in this book – and events which is an advanced topic. When you do something to a control it triggers an event. You can catch these events and use programming code to make changes to the database.

I'm not going to go into the detail of that but I think it's important that you know that it exists because when you get into advanced problems the knowledge will be a life saver.

But, for now, there are two fields that we want to change.

The first of these is the actual text that the Label is showing. Click onto the combo box for Label

And change it to the text that you want the label to show:

Watch as the label text changes on the form when you press enter.

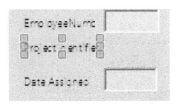

Changing the Name of a control

Right at the top of the properties dialogue is a name field

Name............................... Label Field 1

Each control, label and element of a form has a name. While this isn't visible as far as the end user is concerned when referring to the element (either in code, or when using another element of the form) it's very useful to have a name that you can remember.

I like to use the prefix lb for label, and then something meaningful:

Name............................... lbProjectID

Visibility, Printability and Enable properties

Sometimes there is a control in a form that you don't want the end user to see. If you want to hide a control, simply change visibility from Yes to No

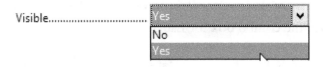

Similarly if there is a control you don't want to print change

Printable from yes to no:

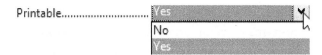

If you want a control to be visible but not editable by the end user, use the Enabled property:

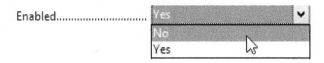

Changing the appearance of the label

To change the font of the label click on the button beside the font

You'll see a font change dialogue that allows you to set the font to whatever you want.

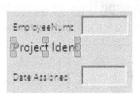

You can change the alignment by clicking on that property:

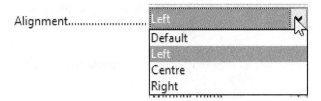

There is also a vertical alignment property, a property that allows you to change the colour of the background and a property called Border that allows you to draw a border around the label. I tend to

find these properties aren't used that often.

Providing Help to end users

Most programs give you information about a control or label when you hover your mouse over them. But when you add a label or control to a form this information isn't very useful. Luckily LibreOffice allows you to control the information that is displayed using the Help text property. Change it and the end user will get a hint about what the control or label is for when they hover the mouse over it.

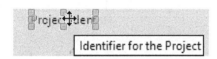

Will display as:

Project Identifier
Identifier for the Project

Move a control or label

You move a control by clicking and holding the mouse and then dragging it to wherever you want in the document. You can resize it by clicking on it and dragging the rectangles to the proper place. This is the same as most other user interfaces for things like word processors or spreadsheets.

More on controls

So far we've dealt with the simplest control in a form – the label. But there are a lot more controls that are available for use in the Form Design view. These include list boxes, combo boxes, text fields and more.

They give you a large degree of power when you're making a form.

We've come across controls every time we make a form in the Form Wizard. For example, if you want to make a form that updates a text field you'll have entered the information into a text box.

Adding a control to the form

Say you want to add a combo box to the form. Simply go to the combo box icon on the left hand side, click it then move the mouse to the place on the form where you want to add the combo box. Click and hold the mouse, then move it to where you want the opposite corner of the control to be. You'll see a blue box appear which will show you the dimensions of the control:

When you let go the combo box will appear:

Note that at the moment you'll have a default combo box. I've already shown you how to change the Name of a control and I really suggest that you do that again. I tend to use the prefix cb before combo box:

(Hint: it's in the control properties).

Binding a label to a Field

When you create a control you'll generally also create a label. It can be useful to connect these together. This means that LibreOffice base associates them with each other so you can't delete one without the other etc.

To do this click on the little box besides the label field property:

You'll see a selection dialogue. Click on the appropriate label

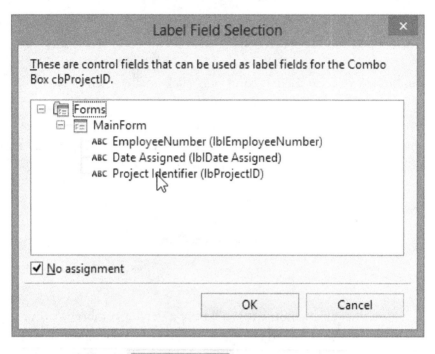

And then press .

You'll see the Label Field change:

Now, back on the form click onto the label, hold shift down and click onto the control too. This will select both the label and the control.

Right click on the control, hover your mouse over Group, and then click on Group:

This means that LibreOffice will allow you to resize, delete and move both items at the same time. If you want to ungroup them, right click on either the label or the control and hover your mouse over group and select ungroup. You can also edit the group without ungrouping them using edit group.

You should only group the label and the control together when you're sure you're not going to edit either further. It will prevent you changing the properties of individual controls.

Filling a combo box with data

The combo box that we just created is empty. In order to make it easier for someone to change the field it's very useful if you can populate controls like comboboxes, listboxes and so on with data from a table.

In the properties dialogue select data:

Then click on the list content field, and select the table or query that contains the data that you're interested in:

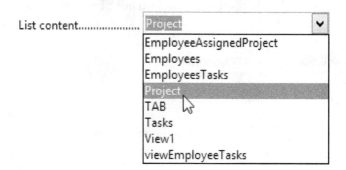

Once you've done that, you can select the field that you want to populate the combobox with in the Data Field option:

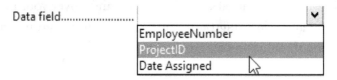

You'll notice that when you run the form the combo box will change so that it contains the data.

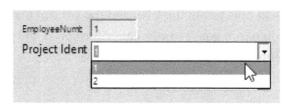

Binding a control to a field

There's a thing to note about this. Although the combobox has data in it, the data isn't linked to your database in any way. You can use an unbound control as input to a query but if you change the information in it this won't have any impact on your database.

To have an impact on your database you need to bind the control to a field.

The first thing to do is to check what table your form is bound to. Click on 🖳 in the taskbar at the bottom of the main viewing area.

You'll see a property dialogue that says Form Properties. Click onto Data General Data Events .

Check that the content field is the table you want to update when you change the data in control.

Assuming it is, go back to the data properties of the Control. The Data Field is the one that binds the control to a field in the table that you're editing. Click on the field you want to bind it to.

Data field........................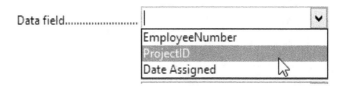

Congratulations. When you change the content of the form you'll also update the database.

There's a problem, though. When a combo box is changed it doesn't automatically refresh the form. So, we're going to need another control to do that for you.

Using a button to refresh the form

When we want the user to be able to do something like delete a record or refresh a form it can be useful to give them a button they can press. LibreOffice has a button control that you can use to do precisely that.

In the list of controls on the left hand side of the screen click the push button icon [OK] . Then draw the button onto your form in the same way you put the combo box onto the form. Remember the blue rectangle shows you where the button will be:

Once you draw it, you'll see the default push button

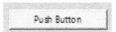

You can change the label in the control properties just link a combo box

Label.. | Refresh form ▼ |

And you can also change the controls name:

Name.. | btnRefreshForm |

In fact you can change alignment, font, colour and so on just like a combo box.

There's one major thing that's different. In the properties list there is a field called Action which gives you the ability to run standard actions

Action............................... | None ▼ |

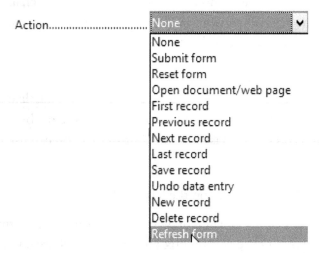

None
Submit form
Reset form
Open document/web page
First record
Previous record
Next record
Last record
Save record
Undo data entry
New record
Delete record
Refresh form

In this case we're going to give the button a Refresh form action.

But note that there are a lot of other actions. One to note is the Undo data entry which allows you to change your mind when entering data into a form. Submit form gives an implicit commit so that you can't change your mind, as does save record. There are other options for navigation but they are all self-explanatory.

Formatted Field

Sometimes you may want to control the format of a field. This allows you to:

- Control how data is entered
- Display things like unit, explanatory text or similar,
- Choose how dates are displayed and so on.

You can do this with the Formatted Field control %F . Draw it onto the form like any other control, then there are several properties that are important to consider. The first is the max text length which you will need to increase to the size of the field:

Max. text length................ 0

You can also set the maximum, minimum and default values for the field if it's a number

Value min.............................

Value max.............................

Default value........................

One of the most interesting fields is the Formatting field:

Formatting...........................

You can either type in the formatting code directly (information on custom format codes can be found at https://help.libreoffice.org/Common/Number_Format_Codes or use one of the standard formats by clicking on the ... .

This brings up a dialogue that allows you to use predefined formats for numbers, percent currency etc. I find that for most purposes these predefined formats are perfectly adequate and you don't necessarily need to go into the detail of custom format codes most of the time.

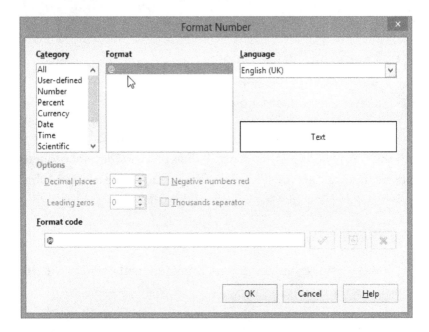

Controlling tabulation

When you press tab (and sometimes enter depending on the control) LibreOffice moves you to the next control in the form. Sometimes, though, you may want to control the next item that appears in a form or stop anyone tabbing onto a control.

The ability to set these parameters is available in almost all controls by setting the Tab Stop property to yes if you want it possible to tab onto the control, or no if you want tab to bypass the control.

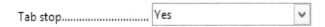

You can control the order by clicking on the rectangle next to tab order

Which brings up the Tab Order dialogue. Note that the **Automatic Sort** button means that LibreOffice will try to

determine the order you're most likely to want, whereas by selecting a field and clicking [Move Up] or [Move Down] you can manually change the order.

In the past we've discussed how to name controls but this is an example of when naming controls logically really does help. As you get a larger form the default names can be close to incomprehensible:

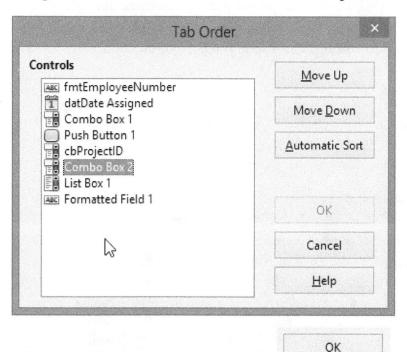

Once you're happy with your choices click [OK] .

Other Controls

Obviously we've already looked at a number of controls, but the control bar doesn't have all the controls that you might want to use

in it – you can click on the more controls or all the fields.

Several of these additional controls are for things like navigation, grouping objects together, and Date and Time. There's also an image control.

One thing to note is that with the image control it's important to bind the control to a field in your database, otherwise you're very likely to lose any information you put into the control when you close the form.

There's a lot of ground to cover with these controls and because they regularly change I'd suggest accessing the help documentation at https://help.libreoffice.org/Common/More_Controls if you have any problems using these fields.

Events and Macros

While we've dealt with many of the basic functions of LibreOffice that you might expect to use every day, events comes far more into the category of very powerful techniques. In essence, events give you the ability to program LibreOffice to do almost anything that a modern programming language is capable of.

Say you have created a Push Button control, and you want it to do something when you click on it. We've already shown you some basic actions that LibreOffice supplies. But if you click on Events in the properties dialogue you see that it's possible to control what happens when you do all sorts of things to the control:

For example, when focus is given to the button the "When receiving focus "event is triggered. When the mouse is moved the "Mouse moved" event is triggered. If someone clicks on the button the "Mouse button pressed" event is triggered.

You can get a list of the meanings of events from https://help.libreoffice.org/Common/Events_2 .

The events trigger macros that you select by clicking the [...] to the right of the event. When you're selecting a macro you first see the Assign Action dialogue:

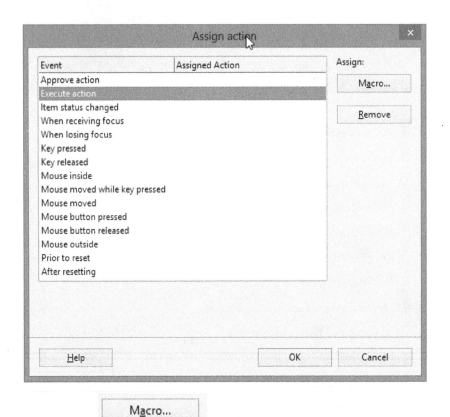

Click on  o assign the macro.

On the left hand side you see a list of Library's. This contains macros you've made yourself (My Macros), macros that are already in the current database (in this case, Staff.odb) and LibreOffice Macros which are standard LibreOffice macros:

Library
- ⊞ 🖙 My Macros
- ⊞ 🖙 LibreOffice Macros
- ⊞ 📄 Staff.odb

If you expand LibreOffice macros by clicking on it ⊞ 🖙 LibreOffice Macros on the right hand side you'll see further subcategories.

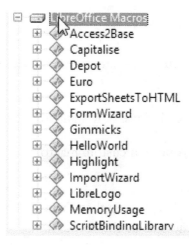

Say you wanted a word count macro, scroll down until you get to 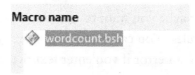 and click on it. On the right hand side are a list of macros available.

Double click on the macro that you want. You'll see in the Assign Action dialogue the macro has now been associated with the event:

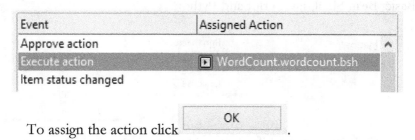

To assign the action click OK.

All this seems very complicated at the moment doesn't it? A bit of an odd way to go about things. But the reality is that it gives you a very fine control over what LibreOffice offers because you can set

Macros to happen given almost any event that can happen to the form.

And you don't need to use only standard macros.

You can create your own custom macro.

The Macro Organiser

Before going further, I guess that it's important to realise that we're going a long way outside the scope of this book. This book is a beginner's book, and macros are really quite an advanced technique.

Macros are in essence bits of custom code that you run when appropriate that allow you to automate things in your database.

For example, maybe you want to custom validate a field using complex business rules. You can write a small program that will do precisely that, giving an error if you enter text that's wrong.

You can organise macros by hovering your mouse over macros in the tool menu, then organise macros and the programming language that you want to use. LibreOffice supports LibreOffice Basic, Bean Shell, JavaScript and Python.

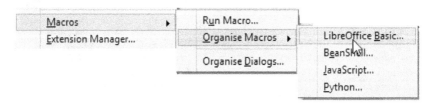

This brings up the LibreOffice Macros window, which allows you to run a macro, assign a macro to an event, edit a macro, delete or run the organiser:

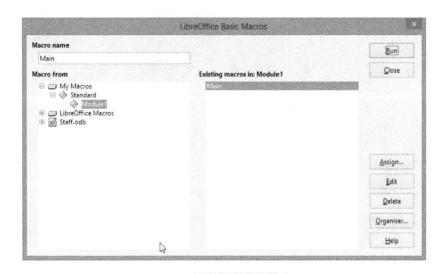

Note that if you click on 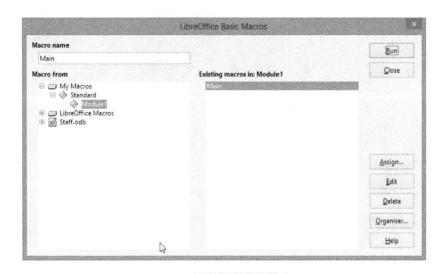 this will bring up the Macro Organiser that will allow you to create a new macro:

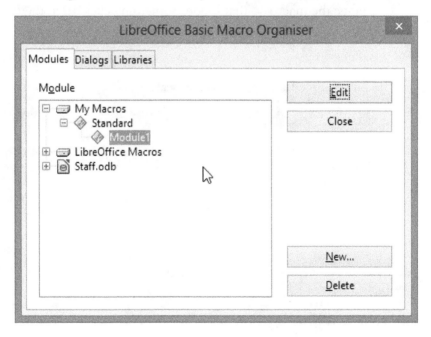

Click on New... to create the new macro. You'll be asked to supply a name:

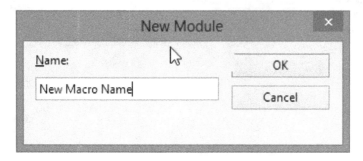

And when you click OK it'll show up on the list.

To change the macro so that it does something click on it, then

click  .

The LibreOffice Basic editor will appear.

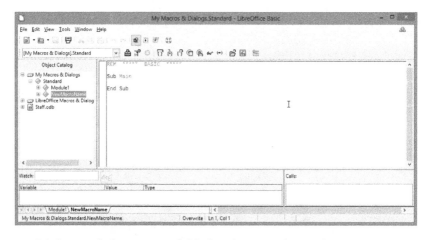

It's beyond the scope of this book to teach you how to program in LibreOffice Basic, but you can find out more from https://help.libreoffice.org/Basic/Programming_with_Basic and https://help.libreoffice.org/Basic/Basic_Help

More information

We've covered a lot of ground in this chapter, but Form Design is an advanced subject. You can get more information on form design from the LibreOffice Base handbook available from http://www.libreoffice.org/get-help/documentation/ .

Next Chapter

In this chapter we've covered a lot of information on Form design.

The next chapter will focus on how to get information out of the Database, in particular Reports – the final major part of LibreOffice Base.

.

6 REPORTS

Once you've created a database you'll often want to get the same information out of it. For example, in an accounts database you'll want a report on invoices that have been paid or unpaid. Creating a report allows you to get information out of the database in a format that is appealing and useful.

You can create Reports from Views, Tables and Queries in the same way that you can create Forms, although it is very common for people to create Reports primarily from queries.

Fortunately, creating a report from a query is very easy to do

Creating a Report using the Wizard

The first step is to create a query that produces the information you want to display. I've shown you how to create a query in earlier chapters.

Once you have the query written running the Report Wizard is

simple. Click on   Queries   in the databases dockable window. Then, right click on the Query that you want to turn into a report in the query dockable window and click on Report Wizard:

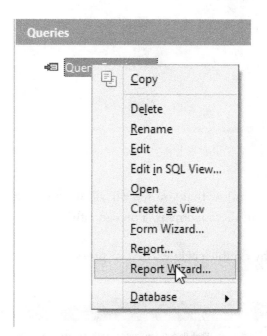

This will start up the Report Wizard window. Notice that behind the report window is the Oracle Report Builder which LibreOffice uses in a similar way to the Query Design or Form Design window.

You can see a preview of the report that you are making in the Oracle Report Builder window which refreshes each time you click Next.

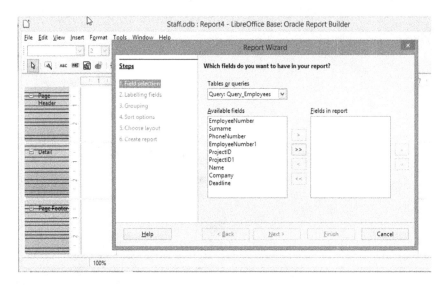

Field Selection

The first window that you see will allow you to choose the fields that you want in the document. You can either select each field

individually by double clicking on it or press 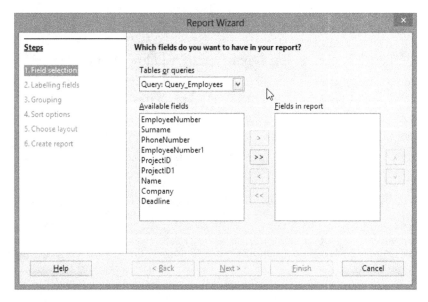 to select them all.

Like previous wizards if you double click on a field you've

selected in the Fields in Report list it'll remove the field. Or you can click 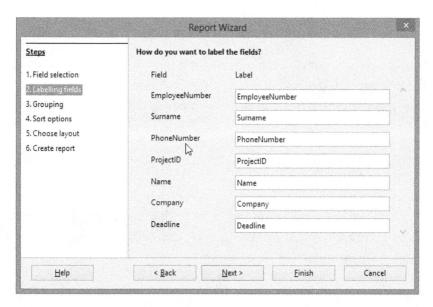 to clear the entire box.

Note that in the above example you don't need to show EmployeeNumber1 or ProjectID1.

Once you're happy click [Next >] .

Labelling Fields

We've already come across the idea of aliases in the Query Design window. The next window allows you to control the labels in the form:

It's pretty self-explanatory. For example

| EmployeeNumber | Employee Identification Number |

Will give EmployeeNumber an English-language label.

Once you're happy click [Next >] .

Grouping

Grouping is a hard concept to explain but when you see it, it becomes obvious. If you were to Group this report by EmployeeNumber

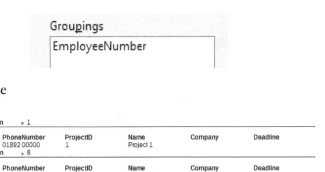

You'd see

Employee Identification	▸ 1					
Surname	PhoneNumber	ProjectID	Name	Company	Deadline
Ecclestone	01892 00000	1	Project 1		

Employee Identification	▸ 8					
Surname	PhoneNumber	ProjectID	Name	Company	Deadline
		1	Project 1		

So, if there were multiple items for EmployeeNumber, you'd see them grouped together. This can be useful if, for example, you want to see all the expenses incurred by each employee in your company.

Once you're happy click 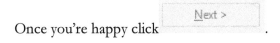 .

Sort Options

If you select a field to group by in the last window you'll see that it's automatically sorted by although you can chose the Ascending or Descending option.

Sort by

EmployeeNumber

◉ Ascending
◯ Descending

You can then chose other fields to sort by. So, in the following example you'd sort by EmployeeNumber and then Surname

If you have multiple items with the same EmployeeNumber, LibreOffice Base would sort by the next field on the list.

Once you're happy click Next > .

Chose Layout

The next window allows you to choose layout. I often just go with Tabular since I prefer it. You can also chose the orientation of the reports (i.e. whether the paper will be printed in landscape or portrait).

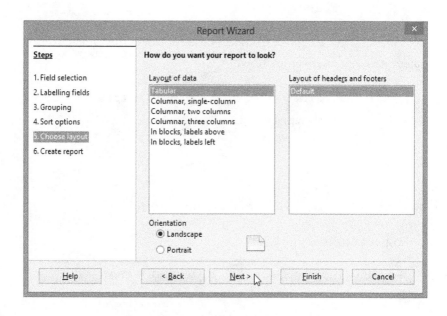

I tend to keep the default option in this page of the wizard but that is a matter of taste. Experiment and see what you like. Once you're happy click  .

Create Report

The next window allows you to create the report.

You can chose to change the title of the report

Title of report

Query_Employees3

The next option allows you to choose whether to create a static report which shows the data at the time the report was made, or a dynamic report which updates every time the report is opened.

What kind of report do you want to create?
- Static report
- Dynamic report

Finally, you can chose to modify the report in the Oracle Report Builder or create the report now.

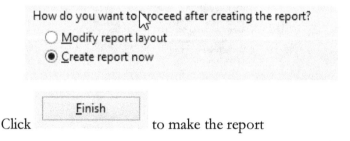

How do you want to proceed after creating the report?
- Modify report layout
- Create report now

Click [Finish] to make the report

Printing a report or exporting it to pdf

To print a report click on 🖶 . If you want a preview first click on 📄 .

To export a report to pdf click ![PDF] . You'll see a save as dialogue. Choose where to save the file to, and click Save .

Finding an Item in a report

You'll see a Find box at the bottom of the report screen. Type in the text that you want to find

And press enter. LibreOffice may ask you if you want to start at the beginning, in which case select yet. You'll see the text highlighted in the main report:

Surname	PhoneNumber	ProjectID	Name	Company	Deadline
Ecclestone	01892 00000	1	Project 1		

Employee Identification ▸ 1

Employee Identification ▵ 8

Which can be very useful when you have a very large report.

You can click ⌄ to search down the document, or ⌃ to search up it.

Keeping a copy of a report that you've run

One of the features of a dynamic report is that every time you run it you'll get an up to date report. But often you'll want to keep a copy of a report you make for historical or auditing reasons.

To keep a copy click on Save a Copy... in the File menu. You'll see a save as dialogue. Chose the filename and location, then click save.

Modifying the Report in Oracle Report Builder

As a rule I think it's generally much easier to use the Report Wizard to take most of the effort out of your report writing. However, you'll often want to make modifications in reports such as adding headers, footers, and dates and times.

You can make these changes using the Oracle Report Builder.

To run the builder click on **Reports** in the main Database dockable window, then right click on the Report you want to modify. Select edit.

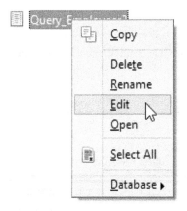

You'll see the Report Builder window open.

Add a Report Title to the header.

If you look at the top of the report in the Builder window you will see a Page Header (Labelled in yellow)

To add a Report title to the header click anywhere on the header to select it. Then hover your mouse over Report Controls in the insert menu and click Label field:

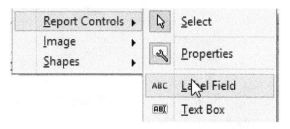

You'll see a label added to the page header:

Click on the label and hold the mouse down, then drag it to wherever you want the title to be on your form. You'll notice that LibreOffice shows you using dotted lines exactly where you are putting the label.

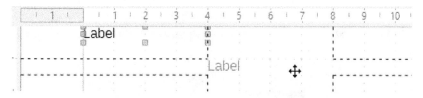

Change the name of the Label in the properties dockable window on the left hand of the screen

Then change the display text of the label

Note that whatever you type in the label field will appear on the form

You can change the font, font size, add emphasis etc. by using the standard icons on the taskbar.

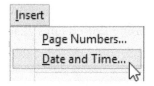

Add a date to the header

In the Insert menu click Date and Time.

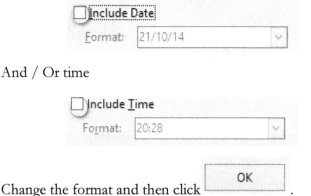

You'll see a dialogue which allows you to include the date (click on the highlighted square)

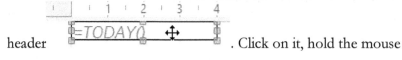

And / Or time

Change the format and then click OK.

You'll see a date or time field appear in the header . Click on it, hold the mouse button and drag and drop it anywhere you want on the form.

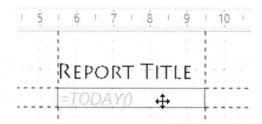

Change the Font or background colour of an field

Sometimes you may want to highlight a particular field. To do so, it can help if you change the font, or change the background colour.

To change the background colour select the field by clicking on it.

In the properties change Background Transparent to No

Then click on the square by font:

In the Character Settings dialogue click on Background

And chose the background colour you want:

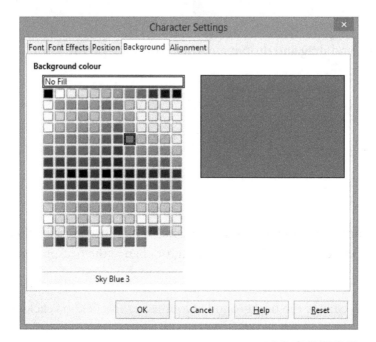

If you don't want to change the font click **OK** otherwise chose the font tab:

And choose the Font, style and size that you want from the list of options, then click **OK** .

Inserting an image from a file

Hover your mouse over Image in the Insert menu then click From File

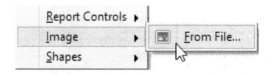

It will open an Insert Image dialogue. Simply go to the directory containing the file you want to insert, and double click on the image.

You can drag and drop or resize the image as necessary.

Insert a field

To insert a field into the report click on

 in the View menu.

You'll see a list of fields in the query or table that you are reporting from. Double click on the relevant field.

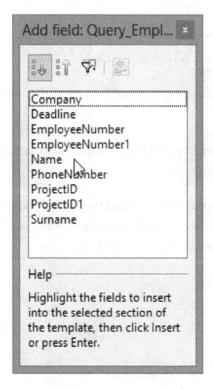

Grouping and Sorting

I don't recommend that you use this option – I find that the Report Wizard works better – but you can change the grouping and sorting options by clicking on 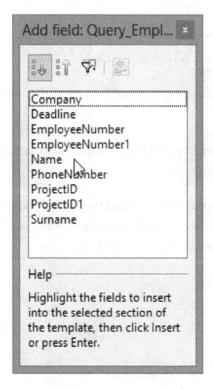 in the view menu.

Running the Report

To see what the report is like click

on  in the Edit Menu.

Next Chapter

In this chapter I've given you some information on how to generate and design reports.

The next chapter will include information on how to use SQL directly in LibreOffice, how to use LibreOffice as a desktop client with other databases and some other thoughts

!

7 GETTING THE MOST OUT OF LIBREOFFICE BASE

While LibreOffice does provide you with an embedded database client one of the most powerful features it has is the ability to use Base as a desktop client that links to databases on other platforms.

This chapter will describe how to use LibreOffice as a client, and it will also go into some miscellaneous areas including how to send SQL directly to the database.

Further to that I'll show you how to import data from Calc to Base, and how to export it to Calc.

Exporting Data to Calc

First create a new spreadsheet by hovering your mouse over new in the File menu and clicking on Spreadsheet

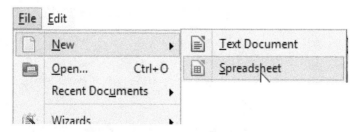

LibreOffice will open a new spreadsheet

In the main LibreOffice window click on Tables to open up the tables dockable window. Right click on the Table that you want to export.

Click on Copy.

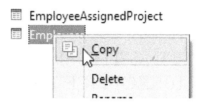

Go to the Calc window. Right click on the first cell that you want the data to appear at:

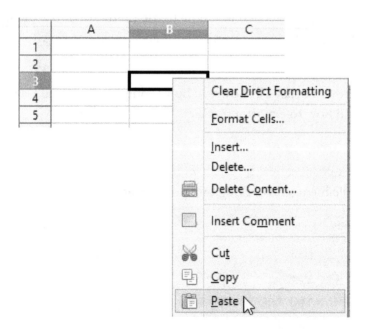

You'll see the data pasted into the spreadsheet:

	A	B	C	D	E	F	G
1							
2							
3		EmployeeNum	Forename	MiddleName	Address	Surname	PhoneNumber
4		1	Thomas	S	29 Nowhere	Ecclestone	01892 00000
5		8	t				
6							

Import Definitions and Data from Calc

When you want to import data from a Calc Spreadsheet it's important to make sure that you are using the correct format. The first row that you import should be Field Names. It's important that these field names are the same as the one that you want your table to contain.

Subsequent rows each relate to one record in the database.

EmployeeNumber	AuthorizedExpenseLimit
1	500
8	250

First, select all the data in calc that you want to copy:

EmployeeNumber	AuthorizedExpenseLimit
1	500
8	250

Right click, and select copy

In the LibreOffice Base window click on Tables then right click in the Tables Dockable Window and click on Paste

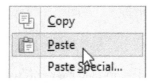

This will open up the Copy Table dialogue.

First name the table

Then make sure you select Definitions and Data

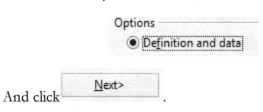

And click Next> .

Select all the fields you want either by double clicking on them individually, or by clicking on 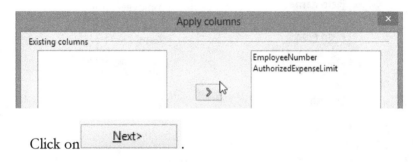 to select them all.

Click on Next> .

The next window allows you to change the definition of each field in turn. Click on each field in turn.

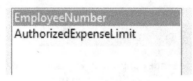

You can change the Field Name, for example to remove spaces where a title has them.

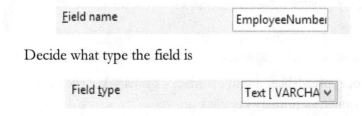

Decide what type the field is

Field type   Text [VARCHA ˅

And also whether you must enter a particular field. If necessary, set the length option for text fields.

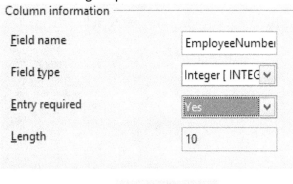

When you're happy click [C̲reate] .

You'll see a warning

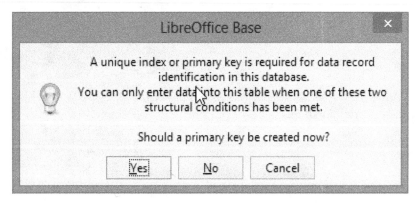

If your spreadsheet doesn't contain a primary key click yes. If it already contains a primary key click no.

You may see warnings like

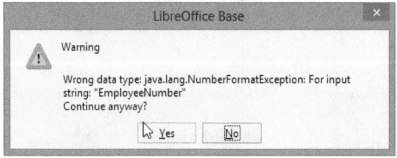

Click on Yes.

If you opted not to create a Primary Key in the last step you'll have to edit the table. Right click on the table that you just created and click Edit

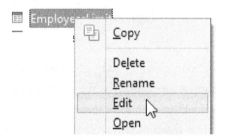

Then add the primary key in the normal way.

You've just imported a table!

Using LibreOffice to connect to an external database

You can use LibreOffice to connect to a spreadsheet, external database or other source of information easily when you create a new database.

When you create a new database the database wizard will give you the option to click on Connect to an existing database

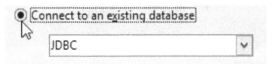

Chose which method you want to use. JDBC is for oracle or Linux based systems, ODBC is for windows based systems. There are options for MySQL and similar database systems.

Because this area of LibreOffice changes very frequently I'm not going to attempt to give you exact directions for the next steps. I think that it's very likely that I'd just get you into trouble by telling you something that might be out of date a few weeks after I write it!

Instead, you can get further information about how to set the parameters for the database connection by clicking on 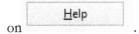 .

One thing I'd like to remind you is the importance of keeping your production environment separate from your development environment. LibreOffice can change database definitions and introduce problems into third party databases. It's important that any development work should be done on a platform that won't risk damaging your main production (i.e. running) database.

Using SQL

So far we've done everything via the GUI – either the query wizard, table wizard, or various design windows. But LibreOffice has to interact with a database to do anything. It does this by generating SQL code which it then sends to the database. Everything, from inserting data into tables to queries and reports accesses the database through SQL.

Sooner or later you're going to come across a problem which the designers of LibreOffice haven't provided a wizard or design widow for. Maybe your SQL query contains subtleties that the GUI can't accurately reflect, or you want to use a specific function of a client database such as validation rules that aren't consistent across all platforms.

Or maybe you just want to do things like create tables or run queries more quickly and efficiently since for a more advanced user it's generally quicker to write code yourself.

For example, it's easy to create a database table with a piece of code in SQL:

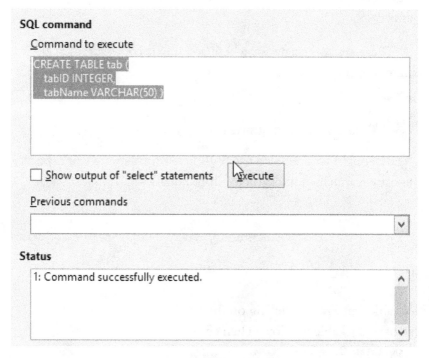

When you execute the command, your database gains a new table:

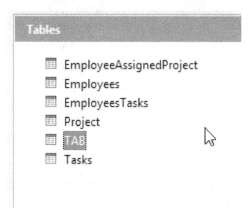

This only takes a few seconds for an experienced SQL programmer, whereas if you go through the wizards it can take a lot longer and may not give you precisely the database definition you want.

There are two scenarios where you might come across SQL commands most frequently:

- **Running an SQL command from the Database GUI**
- **Creating custom queries**

Although, you can also use SQL in subforms, views or reports these are normally done through stored queries.

Using SQL to make custom queries

It's easy to make a custom SQL query. Simply go to the Queries

dockable window by clicking on the Queries button in the database dockable window. Then click on **SQL** Create Query in SQL View...

This will open the Query Design window in SQL view mode.

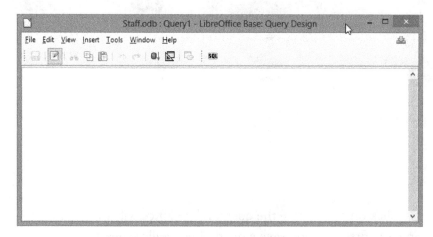

Type in your query into the space provided

Note that it's important that you check the spelling of things like table names, fields and so on.

Click on 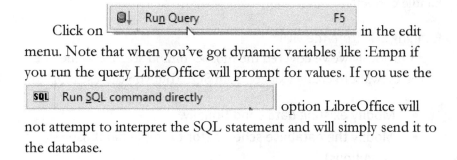 in the edit menu. Note that when you've got dynamic variables like :Empn if you run the query LibreOffice will prompt for values. If you use the

option LibreOffice will not attempt to interpret the SQL statement and will simply send it to the database.

When you run a query LibreOffice Base will send you a preview:

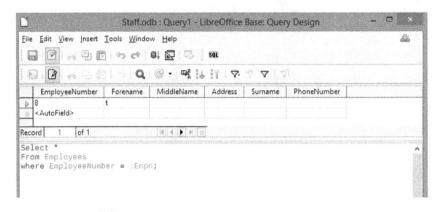

Click on 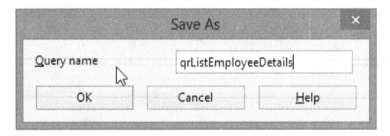 to save the query. LibreOffice will ask you for a name the first time you save a query. I generally suggest giving it something meaningful.

Note that when you create a SQL query via the SQL view this doesn't mean that you can't open it later on using the SQL design view unless the query itself is too complicated for the Design View to handle correctly.

Running SQL from the GUI

Obviously we've covered the most common scenario – the one where we want to create a query from SQL. But you can use SQL to:

- Modify existing data conditionally
- Modify the database schema (for example database definitions)
- And almost anything else that references a database.

To run SQL which isn't a query, click on

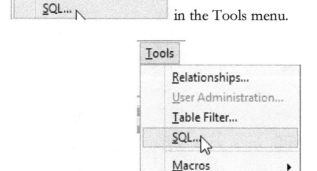 in the Tools menu.

This will bring up the Execute SQL window.

Type the command in the box provided:

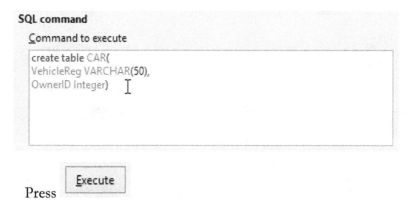

Press

You'll see the result of the statement in the Status window

And you'll also see any output the statement generates in the Output window. For example, the result of a select statement (but when using a select statement remember to check the ☑ Show output of "select" statements option.

Obviously, I've not tried to teach you SQL in this book. There are just too many great resources that already cover the ground such as Sams Teach Yourself SQL in 10 Minutes (4th Edition) by Ben Forta. It's a really interesting area to study, though, and I recommend trying to learn as much SQL as possible if you want to get the most out of LibreOffice Base.

So Long

I've really enjoyed going over the basics of LibreOffice Base. It's a powerful and free platform that allows you to do all sorts of things – from creating a client database to managing your expenses.

I hope that you get a lot out of using it.

As always, you can contact me on thomasecclestone@yahoo.co.uk or on my website at thomasecclestone.co.uk if you have any problems or questions.

And thank you for reading the book!

!

ABOUT THE AUTHOR

Thomas Ecclestone is a software engineer and technical writer who lives in Kent, England. After getting his 1st class honours in software engineering he worked at the National Computing Centre in Manchester, the Manchester Metropolitan University, and for BEC systems Integration before starting his own business in software development. He is a writer who lives on a smallholding in Kent where he looks after a small flock of Hebridean sheep.

www.ingramcontent.com/pod-product-compliance
Lightning Source LLC
Chambersburg PA
CBHW071002050326
40689CB00014B/3459